LS/66
150

A TOWER
BOOK

the reformation ...then and now

CHARLES S. ANDERSON

AUGSBURG PUBLISHING HOUSE
MINNEAPOLIS, MINNESOTA

66-9710

BR305.2
.A53

THE REFORMATION—THEN AND NOW

Copyright © 1966 Augsburg Publishing House

All rights reserved

Scripture quotations are from the Revised Standard Version of the Bible, copyright 1946 and 1952 by the Division of Christian Education of the National Council of Churches

Manufactured in the United States of America

Augustana College Library
Rock Island, Illinois

Foreword

A tower has both height and strength. Grounded in a firm foundation, it provides the opportunity for a full-range perspective and soaring vision. It was in a tower that Luther had the shattering experience of grace which began the Reformation with its insights into the Gospel of God and new freedoms for man.

Volumes in the Tower Books series aspire to this image. They seek to serve the curious and reflective Christian by examining the varied themes of God and man in clear, concise, and interesting (perhaps even sparkling) ways. Committed to the biblical faith, the various authors explore great ideas, reflect on the application of the faith to daily life, transmit the wisdom of inspiring thinkers in the past, suggest new strategy for the church in the world, and open up the Scriptures as honestly and competently as they can.

Each author is different and writes from his own "tower" and in his own style. You, the reader, read against the background of your own experience, of course.

Being a Christian in the modern age is an exciting enterprise. It requires both diligence and knowledge. For this task, we all need the help and counsel of others.

Take and read.

And joy to you!

Kent S. Knutson
Editor, Tower Books

Contents

Preface

Throughout the history of the church, individuals and movements have been concerned with reform. Sometimes the purpose has been to purify church practice and life; at other times the official teachings have been challenged

In sixteenth century Europe the greatest of such reform ventures began and gathered strength. The central figure was the German monk Martin Luther. This brief study will concern itself with this man and some of his contemporaries.

The Reformation is not only a particular movement at a moment in history. It is also an attitude that is willing constantly to reexamine the present, an attitude that seeks to speak the biblical message to each new generation. This little volume will also seek to examine this facet of "Reformation."

C. S. A.

1.

On Elephants and History

Remember the old story about the elephant and the blind men? None of them had ever been in contact with such an animal. Now each was led forward to examine as best he could the beast before him. After touching the elephant with expert fingers, the sightless men were to describe the creature.

The first blind man carefully examined the trunk of the elephant and, noting its suppleness and strength, reported that it was a snake. The next kneaded, squeezed, and pushed at one of the huge legs. He insisted that he felt a large, rough-barked tree. Other members of this company of the blind examined the ears, tail, and other parts of the elephant's anatomy and gave their reports. Needless to say, in no instance was there an accurate or complete picture. Each man reported only on the basis of his own experience and limited examination of the elephant and consequently gave a true, but nevertheless false description!

Interpretations of the Reformation have often been marked by the same sort of problems faced by the blind men in our story. Able men have approached the same basic body of material but have often been so preoccupied with their own points of view or approaches that they have eliminated all others. They have been blinded by all sorts of things. Some have let denominationalism or nationalism color their pictures; others have been unwilling to acknowledge that any way but theirs was adequate, and so offered purely political, economic, social, or psychological interpretations. To others the only way to understand this phenomenon was in a purely religious sense. Such a method sometimes cut off the whole religious upheaval from the world in which it took place. This vacuum approach to history also gave a false picture.

Now it *is* necessary to choose a principle of interpretation in order to write any history. This principle, if properly chosen and correctly used, will help the reader grasp the significance of an otherwise incomprehensible mass of facts. One must always ask, however, whether the method of interpretation does justice to the story itself.

It is our contention that no interpretation of the Reformation that ignores the religious dimension is adequate. This movement was basically religious and concerned with God and the world, and especially with man and his relation to God. We will therefore use this principle of interpretation. There are other possible approaches. In order to illustrate our point and at the same time avoid a completely one-sided picture, let us begin by surveying some of the other prominent approaches.

Princes and Kingdoms

The effect of politics on religion is not new; in fact, the political situation in Europe and particularly in Germany contributed substantially to the preparation of a climate favorable to the Reformation. The loosening of the tight tie between church and state as it had existed under figures like Pope Innocent III (1198-1216) had come about through the prodding of fourteenth-century writers such as Dante, Marsilius of Padua, and William of Occam. Coupled with this was the rise of national consciousness and a breakdown of the seeming solidity of the Holy Roman Empire. Since the year 800 when Charlemagne was crowned in Rome, the "Empire" had encompassed most of the territory of central Europe and had symbolized the unity and peace of the Catholic world. But nations became aware of their own characteristics and histories, and at the same time often grew antagonistic or disdainful of others. As a result, the idea of a unified empire lost strength.

This was an age of strong rulers. Few eras can match the collection of crowned heads that marched across the pages of the sixteenth century: Charles V, the emperor; Henry VIII, much-married king of England; Francis I, arch-opponent of Charles and king of France; Suleiman the Magnificent, the dreaded ruler of the Turks. Some countries, such as England and France, were organized and tightly knit, but Germany was very different. Here a multitude of small states colored the map with almost innumerable hues. Each had its own ruler, and while there were some larger loyalties such as to the Empire and the Catholic Church, the general autonomy of each state was closely guarded by its prince, whether he was secular or ecclesiastical.

This general political climate was of great significance for the Reformation. The decentralization of power in Germany that allowed a minor prince such as Frederic the Wise (Luther's ruler) to follow a course of obstructionism in opposition to both emperor and pope, and the national self-awareness of the Germans to which Luther appealed in the *Address to the German Nobility* cannot be overlooked in any attempt to understand the period. To say, however, that the political scene can explain the whole affair is to apply a principle of interpretation that does not do justice to the entire picture. Much more was involved than the national hostilities of the Germans and Italians. More was at stake than the princes' and the emperor's political power.

Markets and Fairs

Fruitful study has been done regarding the economic conditions of the sixteenth century. The old system of barter declined as a new hard money economy advanced. The roots of a capitalistic system are apparent even before the sixteenth century, and the banking families of Luther's day are evidence of its growth. Some classes such as craftsmen and merchants often prospered in the new currents, while others, notably the farmers, were being swept under by economic change.

It is possible to interpret the Reformation from a purely economic standpoint. From this angle one claims that the princes supported Luther only in order to seize the lands of the church, and that the lower classes were more concerned about freedom from feudal laws and from the tithes and fees of the church than about religious problems. Such an interpretation ignores the facts that the Protestant princes were willing to risk the *loss* of all their holdings for the sake of the religious reform and that the peasants were demanding a return to, not freedom from, their feudal privileges. Certainly there were economic factors mixed in with the others, but to maintain that they were decisive, and that the Reformation was *only* the economic protest of the Germans regarding the flow of their hard money over the Alps to Italy, is to misread the record. Economics played an important role but not an *all*-important one in the great upheaval.

Doctors and Couches

A more recent fad has been to turn the psychiatrist loose on history. In 1957 the president of the American Historical Association suggested that the next order of business was to apply the insights of psychoanalysis to history. There had been some rather crude psychological probing and imagining before, but now the refined methods of this modern science were to be used. To some the results provide the key for understanding the Reformation.

There are serious problems facing the person walking this path. In the case of Luther, for example, there are simply not enough reliable pieces of data from his early life to make the puzzle take shape. One is left in the unenviable position of having to depend upon the reminiscences of an old man, or upon legendary bits and pieces that usually find their source in one of his opponents. In addition, when the religious dimension is overlooked the Reformer is seen only as a person whose egocentricity and "search for identity" spur him on. Such interpretations may result in good psychiatry, but are very poor history. An example is John Osborne's play *Luther,* which is more often a caricature than a study in character. Here, as in other one-sided positions, a useful and valuable tool can serve to obscure the basic significance of the whole.

There are other possibilities, of course. For some, the meaning of the movement is to be seen only in reference to the Renaissance and humanism; to others, in the connection with either the medieval or modern world. A German nationalist may emphasize Luther's contributions to the formulation of German culture, while the religious warrior will stress the necessity or tragedy of the turbulent events, depending upon his own religious loyalty.

To understand fully the great upheaval in the sixteenth century one must be aware of the problems and possibilities already mentioned, but none of these principles or patterns of interpretation is adequate if it ignores the religious element. Although its answers have significance for every area of life, the questions the Reformation asked were not basically political, economic, or social; they were religious. Men sought an understanding of the center of the religious life, the heart of the Christian existence. It is to this understanding that we now turn this study.

The Gathering Storm

The winds of change were blowing in the realm of religion as well as in economics and politics in the years immediately preceding the sixteenth century. Institutions and relationships that had been assumed to be permanent were gradually developing cracks in their seemingly solid fronts.

The papacy itself, the primary symbol of the strength and unity of the church, found itself declining in prestige. The heights of papal power had been reached under Innocent III (1198-1216), who ruled Europe as if it were a monarchy. Within one hundred years a new situation was seen in the inept reign of Boniface VIII (1294-1303). Confronted by the rising claims of national states, notably England and France, Boniface demonstrated that his office had lost much of the power it once held.

Another, more disastrous interlude followed when the papacy became so dominated by the French throne that the seat of papal authority was actually moved from Rome to a town in southern France called Avignon. This period (1305-78) caused great disunity within the church. Europe was divided among nations which either supported or opposed the so-called French popes.

The situation was even further complicated from 1378 to 1409 when rival popes ruled, one set at Avignon, and one at Rome. In 1409 an attempt was made at the Council of Pisa to heal the schism by declaring the rival popes deposed and electing a new leader. Unfortunately the two rival incumbents refused to be ousted, and so there were now three popes, rather than two! Imagine the confusion among the faithful in Europe. To which figure were they to listen? Who really was the leader of the church? American elections and political maneuvering are mild in comparison.

This tragic situation was finally corrected by the Council of Constance (1415-17), but a serious blow had been struck at the notion that the church was unified by the papal office. The picture of papal power, dignity, and wisdom that had developed over the years had been terribly shaken by the confusing division. What were the lay Christians to do and believe when popes and counterpopes hurled condemnations at each other and at the faithful?

This period of confusion produced a whole series of men who argued for various types of ecclesiastical reform. In the fourteenth century John Wyclif of England attacked what he felt to be abuses in the theology and practice of the church. Wyclif also supported the translation of the Bible into English and sent his followers out to preach English sermons in the countryside and towns. His Bohemian disciples, Jerome of Prague and John Hus, carried on the Wyclifite program on the continent. A bit later, in the fifteenth century, the Dominican monk Savonarola tried to reform the church through his fiery preaching and personality in the city of Florence, Italy.

Of greater significance than individual attempts at reform was the conciliar movement. When the papacy was in its greatest confusion during the early years of the schism, some learned men began to doubt the wisdom of allowing the popes to govern the church by themselves. After all, such government had led to the intolerable situation of two and then three papal figures tearing apart the unity of Catholic Europe. Perhaps the way to govern the church was through councils as had been the practice in ancient times, as for example at Nicea. (The Council of Nicea which met in 325 led to the formulation of the Nicene Creed.)

The confusion of the years of division plus the desire for reform in the church led to the calling of several councils which attempted to deal with both problems. The schism was healed when Martin V was elected Pope in 1417, but the desire for reform did not bear any other fruit. The idea of having councils govern the church persisted well into the sixteenth century, although the healing of the schism had put the reins of the church back into papal hands.

One further consideration is important in any discussion of papal fortunes during this period. In the fourteenth and fifteenth centuries a new, secular, this-worldly spirit called the Renaissance had risen to great heights especially in southern Europe. Whatever good effects may be traced to this renewal of classical learning and culture, and there are many (think of the artists like Michelangelo, Raphael, Leonardo da Vinci, etc.), the overall effect on the leaders of the church was not good. They became even more worldly than before, and their claim to fame rests more on their positions as patrons of Renaissance art than on their efforts as the leaders of the church. The spiritual leadership of the faithful, emphasized in our day by figures like John XXIII and Paul VI, was not primary in the minds of the Renaissance popes. The papal concern for this world, present throughout the Middle Ages because of the large land holdings that made the pontiffs secular princes, had been accentuated by the Renaissance.

There were also new currents in the intellectual realm. The theological marriage of faith and reason that had characterized the thirteenth century had been challenged by the theologian Duns Scotus (d. 1308) and then annulled by William of Occam (d. 1349), for whom the ultimate authority was neither reason, nor the church, but the Scripture. People called mystics maintained that knowledge of God and his will was not to come essentially through the mind and reason, but by an immediate indwelling apprehension. The relationship between God and man was not to be regarded as basically ecclesiastical or intellectual, but rather personal

The intellectual endeavor at the start of the sixteenth

century had access to a new set of tools. One offshoot of the Renaissance was the humanistic movement of northern Europe. In an attempt to get back to and understand the heroes of antiquity, the humanists stressed both the history and the primary languages of the past. Their motto was *ad fontes,* "to the sources." When this impulse was transferred to the religious realm, there was a growth of interest in the biblical languages and in the attempt to understand the biblical texts historically and literally. This was a great advance over the artificiality of medieval Bible study where every text was subjected to a whole battery of fanciful interpretations. Now, at least among the humanists and their adherents, an attempt was made to find out what had actually been written, to whom, by whom, and for what purpose. This type of study would have great effect on the reformers. The humanists are also significant because of their consistent calls for reform. They held that renovation of the church would come through a return to the simplicity of the early church and the fathers, and by educating man so that he would become truly human. Their cries for changes in the existing church helped create an atmosphere conducive to actual reform. It was into this situation that the reformers stepped.

2.

The Storm Breaks — Martin Luther

We hold that a man is justified by faith apart from works of law (Rom. 3:28).

This is the very highest worship of God, that we ascribe to Him truthfulness, righteousness and whatever else ought to be ascribed to one who is trusted. Then the soul consents to all His will, then it hallows His name and suffers itself to be dealt with according to God's good pleasure, because, clinging to God's promises, it does not doubt that He, Who is true, just and wise, will do, dispose, and provide all things well *(Treatise on Christian Liberty*, 1520).[1]

In November of 1483 the second of the four sons of Hans and Margaret Luther was born in Eisleben, a small town in north-central Germany. Baptized November eleventh, Saint Martin's day, the infant was given this saint's name. The child grew up in a normal medieval Catholic home, learning both the religion of his day and the superstitions of his family. Martin showed an aptness for study, and in 1501 he entered the University of Erfurt where he earned both the Bachelor and Master of Arts degrees.

The Erfurt period was important to the young student, for during this time his teachers were disciples of a philosopher named William of Occam. One Occamist teaching was later to be the cause of great anxiety for Martin—the notion that a person can, in a sense, repent on his own. It was held necessary that a person "do what lay within him," and then God would be merciful. In other words, God loves those who go through the preliminaries by themselves. This became a special problem for Luther whose habit of critical self-examination never allowed him to assert with certainty that he had indeed done his part. There was always, therefore, the nagging fear that since he had possibly not done enough, God was not gracious toward him. In other words, God condemned him in spite of all he had done.

The time spent at the university may also have influenced Luther with respect to the humanistic movement. While it is doubtful that he ever became a humanist himself, this contact directed him to the sources and stimulated in him a desire for reform and an interest in the biblical languages. These factors were to become of great significance in later years.

In 1505 an odd thing happened. Martin, a promising student, had recently embarked upon both a teaching career at Erfurt and the study of law. For a lawyer the possibilities for advancement were immense. A talented man could hope for a position as counselor in either a secular or church court. Luther was a person to whom success and perhaps, if his father's plans took shape, even a profitable marriage were in view.

The way to the top seemed open: wealth, advancement, prestige, and marriage all seemed within reach. On the verge of all these marvelous possibilities he suddenly entered the Augustinian monastery in Erfurt, thus turning his back on the world.

The event that triggered this change of direction may well have been a traumatic experience in a summer storm that so shook the young man that he vowed to become a monk. The key, however, to his turning away from the world to the monastic life is seen in his own statement that he went to the cloister "to obtain a merciful God by denying self and doing good." This search for a "merciful God" is, indeed, the key to the whole of his own personal development which led in turn to the Reformation itself.

People of Luther's day were convinced, as he was, that they were living on the edge of history, i.e., that the end-time was upon them. Because of this their understanding of God was primarily one of wrath and judgment. Even Christ was commonly pictured as the judge, sitting on a rainbow with sword in hand. One result of such an emphasis was the great increase in devotion to the Virgin Mary by the pious. She represented the principle of heavenly mercy and was believed to intercede with her Son on behalf of the believer. Another result was the frantic search for some means of appeasing this angry God.

By all outward standards Luther seemed to prosper in his new religious life. His monastic superiors described him as "a second Paul called by Christ," and in 1506, after a year as a novice, he took the vows of a monk. In 1512 he was made third in charge of his monastery and three years later was appointed District Vicar, which meant that he had full power over eleven monasteries. His star was rising.

Monasticism was essentially a lay movement, but Martin was ordered to study for the priesthood. In his studies he used the works of Gabriel Biel, another follower of Occam, who maintained that "man is capable of loving God by his own power." All this sounded reasonable to Luther. In fact, he wrote that he read it "with a bleeding heart," and that it "warmed his heart and inspired him." He was still a loyal and enthusiastic Catholic. He was ordained in 1507 and thus was qualified, according to Catholic teaching, to offer or sacrifice Christ in the Eucharist, or Lord's Supper. The enormity of this responsibility always troubled Luther. The legend that he turned to run away at his first mass, however, is very doubtful

After his ordination he was ordered to study theology. It was assumed by his superiors that he would one day become a teacher in his monastic order and in the church. His most important teachers were Occamists, and this system convinced him intellectually, although his spiritual problems were not resolved. By October, 1512, Brother Martin was Doctor Martin, for he had risen through the academic ranks until he was at the top, a teacher in the church. During the course of this academic rise he had been transferred to the new University of Wittenberg. He would spend the rest of his life as a teacher at that institution. Twice a week for thirty years he lectured the students who came to sit at his feet. "In between lectures, so to speak, he attended the deathbed of a world and assisted the birth of a new age."[2]

In spite of outward success the basic religious question that had driven Martin to the walls of the monastery had not been answered. His inner turmoil continued even within the cloister

"How can God be gracious to me?" This was the question that drove Luther the monk deep into trial. As he put it:

> In the monastery, I did not think about women, or gold, or goods, but my heart trembled, and doubted how God could be gracious to me. Then I fell away from faith, and let myself think nothing less than that I had come under the wrath of God, whom I must reconcile with my good works.[3]

Various avenues to peace were tried, but they did not lead to the desired goal. Luther describes it:

> When I was a monk, I tried with all diligence to live according to the Rule, and I used to be contrite, to confess and number off my sins, and often repeated my confession, and sedulously performed my allotted penance. And yet my conscience could never give me certainty, but I always doubted and said, "You did not perform that correctly. You were not contrite enough. You left that out of your confession." The more I tried to remedy an uncertain, weak and afflicted conscience with the traditions of men, the more each day found it more uncertain, weaker, more troubled.[4]

> After watchings, studies, fastings, prayers and other most severe exercises with which as a monk I afflicted myself almost to death, yet that doubt was left in the soul, and I thought, "Who knows whether such things are pleasing to God?"[5]

Even the Sacraments, carefully and frequently received by the troubled brother, did not give the promised peace. They emphasized personal responsibility and action so the question kept plaguing Luther, "What if I have not done enough?"

In short, even within the monastic walls where one was supposed to be living the highest type of Christian life, doing even more than was required by God of the ordinary person, even here Luther's fears continued. These fears centered on the notion of God as unrelenting judge, and upon the demands of the monastic discipline which aimed at perfection (Luther took this theoretical goal as a practical demand). The Occamist notion that one had to "do what lay within him" before God would be merciful and accepting, added to his torment.

His personal failure in fulfilling man's part in salvation and his awareness of the continuing character of his sin led him to question *not the teachings* but *himself*. He came to see sin in terms of self-centeredness and pride, as Paul and Augustine had done before him. The self has absolutely no limits in its grasping. Man does not want God to be God because he himself wants to be God. While all men are subject to this, it is nowhere more rampant than within professional religious groups. Here, as nowhere else, men deceive themselves in regard to their religious and moral attainments; here they shine as liars in their strutting, boasting, and pretending, especially insofar as they are religious and conform to the requirements. Everyone is swept up in this mass self-delusion. As

Luther put it: "Every man is a liar; only God does not lie."

Luther, of course, saw and included himself in this dark picture, and hence could find no peace of mind, for even at the height of apparent humiliation, at the moment of greatest service, there was always the note of pride. He concluded that the fulfillment of the divine commands was impossible because of selfishness. Man, as a created self, cannot fulfill God's law because of his sin.

In 1510 another avenue of relief opened for Luther when he was sent on monastery business to Rome. Here, at the very center of the Catholic world, he expected to find peace. But this was not to be the case. Although he "ran about madly," to use his own words, to acquire as much merit as possible, he was not eased in spirit, but rather troubled by the Italian clergy and by the state of affairs in the Roman church. As he later wrote, "I would never have believed that the papacy was such an abomination, if I had not myself seen the Roman court."[6]

In short, Luther experienced outward progress in his order and in theological studies, but continued to have inner turmoil. Monasticism failed him even though it was the highest form of religious life—and he went all the way in it. Scholasticism, the academic world, failed him and even added to his problem. He was a Doctor of Theology, but still had not found peace. The Roman excursion, a trip to the very center of Roman piety, gave him no help. What could possibly be done? Was there any hope for this troubled monk and teacher?

Light from the Scriptures

The answer came in the course of his studies of the Scripture.

Upon receiving his doctorate Luther embarked upon a course of teaching the Scripture which lasted until his death. Beginning with Genesis, he proceeded to the Psalms in 1513-15, to Romans in 1515-16, to Galatians in 1516-17, to Hebrews in 1517-18, and then to the Psalms again in 1519. It is evident from the records of these early lectures that he was still enmeshed in his own spiritual struggle when he began. He later put it: "When I became a doctor, I did not yet know that we cannot expiate our sins."[7]

The sum total of the picture of God as wrathful judge was captured for Luther in the words the "justice" or "righteousness" of God. The righteousness of God was seen as that quality which God has in and by himself and by which he judges and condemns those who do not measure up to the divine standard. The religious life in this context was living *up* to the command to love, and the *norm* for such a life was the divine perfection and righteousness. Man's life is to be a continual attempt to come up to the divine standard; his striving is a means by which he acquires merit before God.

With this understanding and background it is not surprising that Luther had difficulty with the words "the righteousness of God." He once said, "Wherefore, if I may speak personally, the word 'righteousness' so nauseated me to hear, that I would hardly have been sorry if somebody had made away with me."[8]

Later in his career he reminisced:

> For thus the Holy Fathers who wrote about the Psalms were wont to expound the "justus deus" as that in which he vindicates and punishes, not as that which justifies. So it happened to me as a young man, and even today I am as though terrified when I hear God called "the just."[9]

It is of significance that the very words which epitomized the conflict in Luther's religious life should become the doorway to his new understanding of the life in Christ. The doorway was discovered as he studied and lectured in the Psalms and finally in Romans.

In both Psalms 31 and 71 the same phrase occurs: "In thy righteousness deliver me." If one held to the understanding that God's righteousness is that quality by which he *condemns,* this appeal seemed senseless. The appeal for deliverance is to the very attribute of God which condemns! This puzzled Luther the Bible teacher—and man.

The solution came when he turned to Romans for his lectures and arrived at that section in chapter one where the Apostle had written:

> *For I am not ashamed of the gospel: it is the power of God for salvation to everyone who has faith, to the Jew first and also to the Greek. For in it the righteousness of God is revealed through faith for*

faith; as it is written, "He who through faith is righteous shall live" (Rom. 1:16, 17).

Luther felt drawn to Paul, but this one passage blocked the road; the old confusion persisted until finally, as Luther described it:

> All the while I was absorbed with the passionate desire to get better acquainted with the author of Romans . . . but I stumbled over the words concerning "the righteousness of God revealed in the Gospel." For the concept "God's righteousness" was repulsive to me, as I was accustomed to interpret it according to scholastic philosophy as the "formal or active" righteousness, in which God proves himself righteous in that he punishes the sinner as an unrighteous person . . . until, after days and nights of wrestling with the problem, God finally took pity on me, so that I was able to comprehend the inner connection between the two expressions, "The righteousness of God is revealed in the Gospel" and "The just shall live by faith."

> Then I began to comprehend the "righteousness of God" through which the righteous are saved by God's grace, namely, through faith; that the "righteousness of God" which is revealed through the Gospel was to be understood in a passive sense in which God through mercy justifies man by faith . . . . Now I felt exactly as though I had been born again, and I believed that I had entered paradise through widely opened doors. . . . As violently as I had formerly hated the expression "righteousness of God" so I was now as violently compelled to embrace the new conception of grace and, thus, for me, the expression of the Apostle really opened the gates of paradise.[10]

The implications of this view are manifold.

For one thing the whole past direction of thought

was changed. Salvation is basically a movement of *God to man,* where God is the active figure, and not a movement of man to God, with man as actor. Righteousness is not by law and striving for merit, but rather it is the acceptance of the sinner by God, purely by grace, the favor of God. Luther, following the New Testament, often uses the words "justified" and "justification" to describe this righteousness, this being acceptable to God. This "justification" is by grace through faith. As Paul notes in Romans 3:28, "We hold that a man is justified by faith apart from works of law." This does not mean that law is now destroyed. Both Law and Gospel, demand and promise, are in force, but the theological function of the Law or demand is to humiliate, to drive one to self-accusation, so that the Gospel or promise may be accepted.

Man in this understanding is accepted by being forgiven and in no other way. He is thus enabled to make a new start. Faith is trust in this divine action and promise, and a daring confidence in the act of God. The whole life of the believer is affected by this. He is filled with gratitude so that all things are new and all actions filled with spontaneity.

From this understanding Luther came to assert Christ before all. "Christ is the exemplar of the Christian life." This means that Christ lives out the experience of every Christian. Just as he was humbled only to be raised, so also the believer is humbled, crushed by the Law, so that he may be raised in Christ.

Christ is not only the exemplar of the Christian life, he is also God in action. Because of the absolute centrality of the Christ figure, Luther called this new position the *Fides Christi,* i.e., faith dependent upon, focused upon Christ. Luther's understanding of God is always Christological; he refuses to think about God apart from Christ. God is not to be found by seeking, whether it be by mystical experience or intellectual probing; he is found only where he chooses to be found, in his revelation, in Christ.

Each of the above themes was to be of great significance for Luther and for the reforming efforts which he would make. It is safe to assert that everything that followed was already prefigured in the great discovery about the righteousness of God that took place sometime between 1512 and 1515-16.

The major result of the discovery was the indulgence fight of 1517. It was this controversy that triggered the whole series of events that led to the open split and the Reformation.

The Indulgence Battle

In Roman Catholic understanding, penance is the sacrament in which the believer confesses his sin, receives absolution, and performs certain acts of satisfaction. These "satisfactions" are penalties of a disciplinary nature which the priest has the right to impose. They are temporary, not permanent, can be reduced or increased, and usually take the form of giving alms, fasting, or prayer. The reduction of these penalties by the church is an indulgence. This can be a partial or complete removal of the penalty.

By Luther's day the use of indulgences had ballooned, and many types of abuse had crept into the scheme. For example, they could now be purchased for money and were believed to extend even beyond death. There were several causes for this growth. For one thing there was a persistent demand from the laity; after all, if punishment could be removed in this way, not only from one's self, but also from loved ones now departed, who would hesitate? There was, in addition, the growing need for funds in the church. In retrospect it is plain that not all the funds gathered were used well, but some of the motives were good in themselves. At least part of the money raised by the indulgence which finally roused Luther to action was used in the construction of the largest church in Christendom today, St. Peter's in Rome.

In 1514 or 1515 Luther had, in addition to his other duties, taken on the task of being pastor in the town church in Wittenberg. It was one of those situations where the pastor was ill and someone asked to help out temporarily was eventually requested to stay on. In this capacity Luther became increasingly concerned about the effect of the sale of indulgences on the Christian lives of his parishioners. Indulgences, he felt, led men astray, for they made one fear the penalties, not the sin, encouraged false hopes of salvation, and thus made light of true repentance.

He preached about it, wrote letters to bishops and jurists, and finally wrote to his Archbishop and others, but there was no response at all. Finally, on October

31, 1517, the Ninety-five Theses were posted. This was an act that was to have far-reaching effects.

Outwardly it was not at all impressive. Luther simply tacked up a sheet of paper on what served as the university bulletin board. On the paper was a series of statements upon which he wished to debate. A number of things should be noted: (1) This was completely normal procedure; (2) the church had not acted officially on the points in question and so they were open to debate; (3) Luther had no intention of arousing popular opposition to indulgences, only the educated few could read the Latin in which the statements were presented; (4) Luther himself was not at all clear on all the points, in fact, he later tried to explain some of them and withdraw others.

The central issue of the whole list was not faith, as one might expect, but repentance. The first statement sets the tone for the whole document. "When our Lord Jesus Christ said 'Repent,' he meant that the whole life of the believer should be one of repentance."[11] This is to say that the believer does not concern himself with fleeing from punishment for sin. He does not attempt to limit repentance to particular moments or acts, but rather he realizes that his whole existence before God is to be one of repentance.

Two things should be noted in regard to these statements.

On the one hand, they display Luther's conservatism. He asserts that penance is to be retained as a sacrament, that purgatory exists, and that papal authority is supreme. He believed at this time that the excesses in indulgence preaching came from underlings and insisted, "If, therefore, pardons were preached according to the spirit and mind of the pope, all these doubts would be readily resolved, nay, they would not exist."[12] Luther was to discover, as the controversy developed, that he was wrong in this assumption. The indulgence preaching to which he objected was, in fact, approved by the pope. He was also to conclude that several other conservative emphases in the theses were also incompatible with the Gospel as he had come to understand it.

On the other hand, despite their conservative orientation, the statements or theses still put forth a new understanding of religion. Formerly one's place depended basically upon his relation to the church and its Sacraments. The new understanding, based upon the discovery, was that of direct, personal relationship to God. The church was not necessary as an intermediary. For example, theses 36 and 37 maintain that all with true repentance have forgiveness; thesis 5 asserts that the pope remits only man-made penalties; and theses 56 to 66 hold that the Gospel is the real treasure of the church, and that this treasure is not necessarily doled out by the institutional structure. This is really a new definition of religion, although the word "faith" is not even mentioned.

What happened when these statements became known? Nothing for a few months, but soon publishers translated them into German and the common people were aroused. The document was seen as a protest for which the people had been waiting, and the battle was joined. Luther was drawn from the peace of the lecture hall and monastery into the fray. Soon the issues which he had first presented, i.e. indulgences and their abuse, were forgotten, and the center of the controversy became papal power and the nature of the church. It was on this field that Martin, initially the reluctant reformer, was to study and to debate, and eventually to be driven farther and farther away from the traditional stance until he finally stood alone against both papacy and empire.

Two things should be noted at this point in regard to Luther's attitude toward the Reformation. Both have to do with his place in the whole scheme of things. It was his conviction, first of all, that the entire affair was God's doing. Second, because of this conviction he refused to lay any particular significance to his own actions.

His belief that the word he proclaimed was from God was based on his rediscovery of the Pauline understanding of faith and on his own experience. He insisted that he was "more acted upon than acting"[13] and that if he had known in advance what was in store for him during the conflict, he would doubtless have held back. Looking back on the events of the years of storm, he wrote: "Had I known all in advance, God would have been put to great trouble to bring me to it,"[14] and, "Truly God can drive one mad; I do not know whether now I could be so daring."[15]

All that took place in the turbulence of faith came not by Luther's devices, but by "divine counsel."[16]

This combination of feelings of personal hesitancy and divine guidance is perhaps best expressed in these words:

> God has led me on as if I were a horse and he put blinkers on me that I could not see who came running up upon me . . . . A good deed rarely issues from planning wisdom and cleverness; it must all happen in the vagaries of ignorance.[17]

This understanding that God was at the helm led Luther to depreciate his own actions and authority. Just as Paul had stressed his place as an apostle, so Luther pointed beyond himself to the authority of Christ, who alone should be heard. He, Luther, was only "the unworthy evangelist of our Lord Jesus."[18]

His self-evaluation is marked more by a robust sense of humor than by any striving after authority. To the suggestion that his followers be given his name and called Lutherans, he replied with characteristic vigor:

> Who is this Luther? My teaching is not my own, and I have not been crucified for anyone's sake . . . . Why should it happen to me, miserable stinking bag of worms that I am, that the children of Christ should be called by my name that cannot save anyone? I am not, and do not want to be, anybody's master. Together with the Church, I have the one universal teaching of Christ, who alone is the master of us all.[19]

The reform of the church was God's business in which he, Luther, was only an unworthy instrument. This was the conviction of the reformer.

The Call to Trust

The key word to Luther's understanding of religion is trust. Without this basic quality no one can be thought even to be Christian, and without some understanding of what the reformer meant by this term no one can presume to have any grasp of his position. Our discussion may proceed best if we consider this trust in terms of what it looks to, what it is like, and what it does.[20]

That upon which one places his trust, the point where confidence is required, is the promise of God in Jesus Christ.

During the Middle Ages the notion had been prominent among the schoolmen that through the use of reason one could learn a great deal about God, including the fact that he is love, perfection, and acts reasonably. Natural man, i.e. man seen apart from God, could by his reason draw these conclusions from nature.

Luther rejected this remarkable capability in man as he stands alone. The realm of nature analyzed by reason reveals only a God of wrath. Certainly there are beautiful sunsets, fields of waving grain, and other beauties, but there are also storms, famine, and plagues. The only God that nature consistently shows is a God of wrath and caprice. Reason, perfectly competent in some areas, such as in the everyday matters of civil life, is not capable of reaching up to heaven to pry out the secrets of the divine. God, to such endeavor, is a hidden God, whose actions and purposes are beyond describing or finding out. God dwells "in a tent of darkness" and his hiddenness is not to be probed by speculation.

This inability of "natural" reason to pry out the secrets of God is a part of Luther's whole understanding of the state of mankind. Though created by God for fellowship, man has turned away and is now characterized by rampant self-centeredness that makes all converse with the divine impossible. He is "turned within himself" and wishes to put himself on the throne rather than allowing God to rule. In this proud state of supposed independence from God man also chooses his own way of salvation. He takes his natural knowledge of God's power and being (Rom. 1:19 ff.), and instead of being led by it to Christ, turns it to idolatrous uses. He seeks to barter his way to heaven or to gain divine favor by working out the demands of the Law. None of these devices work, as Luther himself discovered in the monastery, for without God's initiative there can be no relationship at all except one of wrath and judgment.

But the glory of the faith, the reason that there can be faith at all, is that God has not chosen to remain hidden, but has revealed himself in Christ. We must seek God where *he* chooses to be found, and not try to create alternate routes. If we wish to be safe, Luther insists, we must "begin where he began," at the manger.[21]

One knows God because God has chosen to reveal himself, because he is a God who speaks. Luther made much of the concept of God as the one who speaks, before whom the proper response is listening and trust. God makes his will known and reveals himself in the Word.

Luther's understanding of the "Word" is by no means simple. He speaks of it in at least three ways: The Word is Christ, the Bible, and preaching. The three hang together, and are necessary to one another.

> *In the beginning was the Word, and the Word was with God, and the Word was God. He was in the beginning with God; all things were made through him, and without him was not anything made that was made. In him was life, and the life was the light of men. The light shines in the darkness, and the darkness has not overcome it . . . . And the Word became flesh and dwelt among us, full of grace and truth; we have beheld his glory, glory as of the only Son from the Father (John 1:1-5, 14).*

On the basis of John 1, Luther asserted that Christ is the Word, the Revealer of the Father. The Bible is Word because it proclaims Christ who is the mirror of the Father's goodness (Large Catechism).[22]

In Christ God shines through, and one knows him, for here he chooses to be found; otherwise he dwells in a tent of darkness. This idea is presented in many ways. For example, in his *Preface to the Epistles of St. James and St. Jude* Luther wrote:

> What does not teach Christ is not apostolic [normative], even though St. Peter or St. Paul taught it; again, what preaches Christ would be apostolic [normative], even though Judas, Annas, Pilate and Herod did it.[23]

The priority belongs to Christ, not to the Bible; it is the Word because it discloses Christ.

In the lecture notes on Romans the idea is developed further:

> The whole Scripture deals exclusively with Christ, if one looks at its depth, and understands it from within.[24]

This includes the Old Testament, of which Luther wrote: "Here you will find the swaddling clothes and the mangers in which Christ lies, and to which the angel points the shepherds. Simple and little are the swaddling clothes, but dear is the treasure, Christ, that lies in them."[25]

Luther wrote much about the relationship of Christ and the Scripture. We will let him summarize for himself:

> In sum, Christ is the Lord, not the servant, the lord of the Sabbath, of law and of all things. The Scriptures must be understood in favor of Christ, not against him. . . . Therefore, if the adversaries press the Scripture against Christ, we urge Christ against the Scripture.[26]

In other words, even the Scripture, the written word, had to give way before Christ, the Word.

The Bible is the Word of God because it is the revelation by the Holy Spirit. Here Luther picked up and developed an ancient theme: the Holy Spirit is the speaker in the Scripture. He could write, "The Bible is the Holy Spirit's own writing," and, "The Holy Spirit has bound his wisdom, counsel and mystery to the Word and revealed them in the Scripture." Nothing is said about method, the *how* of inspiration, but the authority of the Bible is clearly asserted.

Yet Luther did not make a fetish of this, and was

remarkably free on the whole matter. His attitude toward the Epistle of James is well known: James simply was mistaken and did not understand justification. "James is a Jew who has heard the bell of the Gospel but could not find the clapper."[27] In his lectures on Genesis he comments tartly: "James talks nonsense."[28]

In the third place, the Word is the living Word, it is preaching, for the Word of God is perceived only through hearing.

> Now when God sends forth his holy gospel he deals with us in a twofold manner, first outwardly, then inwardly. Outwardly he deals with us through the oral word of the gospel and through material signs, that is, baptism and the sacrament of the altar. Inwardly he deals with us through the Holy Spirit, faith, and other gifts. But whatever their measure or order the outward factors should and must precede. The inward experience follows and is effected by the outward. God has determined to give the inward to no one except through the outward. For he wants to give no one the Spirit or faith outside of the outward Word and sign instituted by him, as he says in Luke 16 (:29), "Let them hear Moses and the prophets." Accordingly Paul can call baptism a "washing of regeneration" wherein God "richly pours out the Holy Spirit" (Titus 3:5). And the oral gospel "is the power of God for salvation to everyone who has faith" (Rom. 1:16).[29]

God is the *Deus Loquens,* the God who speaks. He speaks to me most clearly in Jesus Christ.

Who is this figure, and what has he done? Christ is God incarnate; he is the veil through which God confronts us; he is the mirror in which we see God. In all of these images Luther stresses the incarnation

and how the divine figures came, emptying himself
to be found in human form (Phil. 2:8). Indeed the
picture of Christ's humbling in life and death and his
resurrection in glory became for Luther the picture of
how God deals with each person. He humbles only
in order to raise up and glorify.

He is also the one who mediates between God
and fallen man, who reconciles the two, and who
atones for sin. He is my Lord, and I have been created
in order that I might live under him and serve him
in everlasting righteousness, innocence, and blessed-
ness.[30] His lordship extends over all the world. Even
the powers of sin, death, and the devil are subject
to him because of his victory at the cross and empty
tomb.

He is also seen as Savior. The Gospel is the pure
promise that what man could never do God has
already done in Christ. It is not another Law, or an
addition to the old, with Christ as a new lawgiver, as
Catholicism held. Luther maintained with fervor that
Christ "is not another Moses," i.e. a giver of Law. He
is Savior.

The only proper response to such a figure and such
a message is trust. Now, what is trust like?

What Faith Is Like

It is possible to think of "faith" in terms of opinion,
knowledge, and acceptance of certain statements.
This was certainly not Luther's understanding. Merely
to know all the facts is far from sufficient, nor is

preaching which is geared to this end satisfactory. As he writes:

> It is not enough nor is it Christian, to preach works, life and words of Christ as historical facts.[31]

Even unbelievers may have this type of "historical faith," but it is of no avail.

> Rather ought Christ to be preached to the end that faith in him may be established, that he may not only be Christ, but be Christ for thee and for me, and that what is said of him and what his name denotes may be effectual in us.[32]

Such preaching tells us why Christ came, what he brought and bestows, and what benefit we have in accepting him. In other words, faith becomes saving when it apprehends Christ, not merely as historical figure, but as Christ for me, and when it sees that he is not only the Savior of the world, but *my* Savior. Faith sees that he died not only for the sins of the world, but for *my* sins, and it commits itself to this person in trust. Neither mere knowledge about, nor agreement with, is called for, but trust and commitment.

The difference between knowledge, agreement, and trust may perhaps be seen in this way. Suppose I wish to be a parachute jumper. I go to a school and learn all about the various parts of the chute, and how each part works; this is knowledge. Then I see other students jump and am finally called upon to decide whether the chutes I have seen working would also work for me, i.e. whether they would support me safely. I review my knowledge and finally agree, "Yes, I guess the chute will hold me up." This is agreement. Now the question is, when does this become trust? You know the answer—when I jump out of the plane. At that point I have committed myself, entrusted myself. This is trust.

So also faith is a leaping out, a committing of oneself; a swimming in seventy thousand fathoms, as the Danish writer Kierkegaard put it; a reaching into a dark tent, as Luther says. It is a daring leap which is not based upon empirical proof, but upon confidence in the one who promises. At times one must even trust in the promiser *in spite* of empirical evidence. Luther never tired of pointing to the faith of Abraham who believed God would give him offspring in spite of his extreme age. What proof did he have? None at all, only the promise of God. And this faith was "reckoned to him as righteousness" (Rom. 4:3).

God often works even under seeming opposites. His grace is at times hidden beneath apparent wrath. For example, the very thought that a horrible instrument like the cross could be a means of merciful action is unreasonable. So also—and this is a consistent theme for Luther—God works through apparent opposites in the life of the Christian. There are continual trials and testings of faith, but the same God is working. He is hidden only for the sake of revealing himself. "Man hides himself in order not to be found; God hides himself in order to reveal."[33]

Faith also is of this hidden nature. It is without empirical proof in spite of the persistent demands of man for such demonstration. One is called to make

the leap, to believe the promises and act upon them
without proof. Although rooted in a historical revelation and directed toward a historical personage, faith
cannot be conclusively validated historically. One
cannot prove either the divinity of Jesus, the trust-
worthiness of his promises, or the historicity of central events such as the resurrection. God is hidden,
even where he is revealed; even Jesus Christ is a
hiding place of God, i.e. the divine is seen in him
only through the eyes of faith.

There is a tension that cannot be resolved between
faith seen as God's gift and man's act. On the one
hand, Luther asserted:

> I believe that by my own reason or strength I can-
> not believe in Jesus Christ, my Lord, or come to
> him. But the Holy Spirit has called me through
> the Gospel. . . .[34]

And yet, on the other hand, he insisted that no one
could believe for me. It is the *personal* act of the believer. "If you believe, you have," he insisted. That is,
only if you personally commit *yourself* to the person
and promises of Christ, are they yours.[35]

Only if God has acted in his grace is there the
possibility of such a faith. And yet the individual must
decide and act.

> You yourself must decide; your neck is at stake.
> Therefore, unless God says to your own heart: This
> is God's word, you cannot comprehend it. . . . If
> you do not feel it, you do not have faith, but the
> word merely hangs in your ears and floats on your
> tongue as foam lies on the waters.[36]

The great concern for asserting that God is responsible for all of man's good, including his salvation, prevented Luther from saying that man's part in faith was in any sense meritorious. The glory is God's in every sense. Man's response only accepts what God has done. Now, what is it that he has done, or to put it another way, what does faith do or acquire for the believer?

What Faith Does

Strictly speaking, faith does nothing; it merely accepts what God has done. It is an attitude of receptivity; it is living in a personal relationship with the Lord, a relationship of trust and dependence. But understanding this, what accompanies faith? What happens when one lives in this relationship of trust and dependence?

In his *Treatise on Christian Liberty*,[37] written in 1520, Luther suggests a number of things. For one thing, such a faith justifies. It is the means by which I apprehend and take to myself the righteousness which God purposes to give me in Christ. "Christian righteousness consists of two things; that is to say, in faith of the heart, and in God's imputation."[38]

God gives faith and then accounts it as being perfect, even though we remain sinful and are not perfect.[39] When he speaks of imputation Luther does not refer only to the accounting of Christ's righteousness as the believer's, or to the purely legal picture of not counting sin. He sees sin as a continual ferment and problem in the believer, and when it is not imputed, this means that the power of this sin is held in check.

The believer is never without sin in this life, but he lives "at the same time sinner and justified." Luther defines the Christian at one point: "The Christian is not he who has no sin, or feels no sin, but he to whom God does not account his sin because of his faith in Christ."[40] Luther's picture of justification includes more than the law court and counting house (imputation, reckoning). He also emphasizes the reality of the new life in which the believer has a living relationship with Christ. Here is a righteousness within, for Christ is there.

Faith, secondly, fulfills the commands of God. These commands direct us to the very highest worship of God. Since faith ascribes to him truthfulness, righteousness, and whatever else ought to be ascribed to one who is trusted,[41] it follows that faith fulfills the commands, for this trusting is precisely what is commanded. "For it is a further function of faith, that whom it trusts it also honors with the most reverent and high regard, since it considers him truthful and trustworthy."[42]

In contrast to this attitude, *not* to believe God is the greatest rebellion and wickedness. "For what is this but to make God a liar or to doubt that he is truthful?"[43]

The third, "incomparable benefit of faith is this, that it unites the soul with Christ as a bride is united with her bridegroom."[44] The image of the "royal marriage" is one of Luther's most beautiful. In faith the believer is so united with Christ that all they have they hold in common. This is to say that all that is

Christ's—his righteousness, his good, his glory—becomes mine, and all that is mine—my sin, my unbelief, my guilt—becomes his. We are now so united that a new life is mine in which I am freed from the demands of Law to live in the freedom of responsive love. This union with Christ also unites me with others who belong to the Lord. This unity with others is the church which is gathered around the Word.

Faith also equips us for life in the world. One of the first charges raised against Luther was that by his teaching that man is justified, i.e. accepted by God through faith, the basis for morality and good works was destroyed. After all, it was reasoned, who will endow the hospitals, feed the sick, and the like, if there is no merit connected with these acts?

Luther answered by insisting that a faith that is real *will* produce works, not in order to be accepted by God—this has already happened by the sheer grace of God—but simply because it is of the nature of faith to be living, busy, and active. No one need tell a healthy fruit tree to bear fruit, nor married folk who love each other how they should act toward each other. So also the person who is living in a faith relationship with his Lord will indeed act in such a way, he will bring forth fruit, he will act in love.

The Christian's attitude toward his neighbor is characteristically summarized by Luther:

> From faith flows love and joy in the Lord, and from love a joyful, willing and free mind that serves one's neighbors willingly and takes no account of gratitude or ingratitude, of praise or blame, of gain or loss. For a man does not serve that he may put

men under obligations, he does not distinguish between friends and enemies, nor does he anticipate their thankfulness or unthankfulness, but most freely and willingly he spends himself and all that he has, whether he wastes all on the thankless or whether he gains a reward. . . . As our heavenly father has in Christ freely come to our help, we also ought freely to help our neighbor through our body and its works, and each should become as it were a Christ to the other, that we may be Christs to one another and Christ may be the same in all; that is, that we may be truly Christians.[45]

The reformer could also speak of ethical action on the level of the civil community. God rules here also, but through law. Here one may attain to a "civil righteousness" as he is guided by reason in obedience to law. Our concern has been with the specifically theological dimension. Here all is dependent upon the relationship of trust between the believer and his Lord. This is why it is true that Luther's was a religion of trust.

Footnotes

[1] *Works of Martin Luther* (6 Vols.; Philadelphia: Muhlenberg Press, 1930-43), II, 319. Further references to this edition will be abbreviated as W.M.L.

[2] Gordon Rupp, *Luther's Progress to the Diet of Worms* (London: SCM Press Ltd., 1951), p. 25.

[3] *D. Martin Luther's Works, Kritische Gesamtausgabe* (Weimar: H. Böhlau, 1883-1948), 47,590,6. Later references to this collection will be cited as W.A.

[4] Ibid., 40 II, 15, 15; 40 I, 615, 6; 26, 12, 12.

[5] Ibid., 41 II, 414, 15.

[6] *Ibid.*, 47, 432, 28.

[7] *Ibid.*, 45, 86, 18.

[8] Otto Scheel, *Dokumente zu Luthers Entwicklung* (Tübingen: J. C. B. Mohr, 1930), p. 12.

[9] *Ibid.*, p. 237

[10] W.A., 54, 179-98.

[11] W.M.L., I, 29.

[12] *Ibid.*, 38.

[13] W.A., *Briefe,* 11.39. This statement and the six that follow are cited in Wilhelm Pauck's *The Heritage of the Reformation* (Glencoe, Ill.: Glencoe Free Press, 1961), pp. 20-47.

[14] *Ibid., Tischreden,* 1, 42, 17.

[15] W.A., 6, 157.

[16] *Ibid., Tischreden,* 4, 25, No. 3944.

[17] *Ibid.,* 1, 176, 15.

[18] W.A., 30 III, 366.

[19] *Ibid.,* 8,685,6.

[20] I first heard the words trust, obedience, and discipleship presented as keys to Luther, Calvin, and the Anabaptists respectively in three lectures given by Wilhelm Pauck at Luther Seminary in 1959. In this and innumerable other areas I am indebted to Dr Pauck, my teacher at Union Theological Seminary, New York.

[21] W.A., 40 I, 78, 10.

[22] The Large Catechism. See *Book of Concord,* trans. and ed T. Tappert (Philadelphia: Muhlenberg Press, 1959), pp. 358-461.

[23] W.M.L., VI, 478.

[24] W.A., 56, 414.

[25] W.M.L., VI, 368.

[26] W.A., 39 I, 47, 1.

[27] *Ibid., Tischreden,* 5, 157, No. 5443, and 414, No. 5974.

[28] W.A., 43,231,39.

[29] *Luther's Works,* Vol. 40, ed. Helmut Lehmann (Philadelphia: Fortress Press, 1958), p. 146.

[30] The Small Catechism. See *Book of Concord, op. cit.,* p. 349.

[31] W.M.L., II, 326.

[32] *Ibid.*

[33] W.A., 1,138,13.

[34] *Small Catechism, Book of Concord, op. cit.,* p. 345.

[35] W.A., 18, 118.

[36] *Ibid.,* 10 IB, 335.

[37] W.M.L., II, p. 297.

[38] Luther, *Commentary on Galatians* (London: J. Clarke, 1953), p. 223.

[39] *Ibid.,* p. 225.

[40] *Ibid.,* p. 138.

[41] W.M.L., II, 319.

[42] *Ibid.*

[43] *Ibid.*

[44] *Ibid.,* p. 320.

[45] *Ibid.,* p. 338.

3.

The Storm Moves South —John Calvin

Now therefore, if you will obey my voice and keep my covenant, you shall be my own possession among all people; for all the earth is mine, and you shall be to me a kingdom of priests and a holy nation (Ex. 19:5, 6)

Nothing is so pleasing to God as obedience.[1]

One should not assume that the only area of Europe concerned with reform in the church was Germany. While one must grant that the initial impulse came from the small university of Wittenberg and from Luther, its Bible-oriented professor, still the waves set up by this initial disturbance soon spread far and wide. In this brief study it is impossible to discuss all of the major figures and movements. For example, we should look first to Ulrich Zwingli, Luther's contemporary, who led the quest for reform in German-speaking Switzerland. Though closely related to Luther in many ways, he is remembered most for the things that separated them. A different understanding of the Lord's Supper led to an attempt at agreement at Marburg (1529). This venture failed and could not be pursued due to Zwingli's death in 1531. He died on the field of battle, fighting for the cause of reform. We cannot even stop to try to come to grips with Zwingli, but we must turn to the greatest figure in the Swiss Reformation, a man whose influence has spread around the world, John Calvin.

The Second Generation

Calvin was a second-generation reformer. When he was born in 1509 in a small town about sixty miles northeast of Paris, Luther was twenty-six, and Zwingli twenty-five. By the time he reached maturity, the first great battles had already been fought and the groundbreaking treatises already written. The main lines of the Reformation had already been drawn. His role in the great drama was not that of a prophet, breaking new ground; he was rather a systematizer and organizer whose talents were greatly in demand if the Reformation was to survive. His major contribution is his monumental *Institutes of the Christian Religion,* the greatest systematic presentation of the Reformation position to come out of the sixteenth century. This work is a combination of ideas, drawn from different sources, welded together in Calvin's own style and bearing the mark of his particular genius.

Our concern is not with biography, but with the positions advocated by major individuals and movements. It would be profitable, however, to spend just a few moments on Calvin's development so that we can better see how his position came into being.

Calvin's educational program falls into two main periods. During his early years, up to 1528 when his undergraduate work ended, he was engaged in studies which were designed to equip him for the priesthood in the Roman Catholic Church. Part of this education was paid by grants from the church, probably arranged by the lad's father, a minor church official in his home town in France.

The young man turned from theological studies, however, when his father fell out of favor with the church officials and ordered his son to switch to the study of law. The obedient youth followed his father's orders and studied at Orleans and Bourges, famous French schools of law. He became a Doctor of Law in 1532.

During both these early periods Calvin was under the influence of noted humanists. We have already discussed this movement and its relation to reform. It generally created a climate favorable for change by its concern for the biblical languages and for the purification of the church. Calvin's real love was not law but the study of ancient culture, language, and literature. His first literary venture was commentary on one of the writings of the Roman philosopher and playwright Seneca (d. 65 A.D.). It was a typically humanistic product

At the same time that the young man was progressing educationally, he was also developing in a religious sense. Starting as a loyal son of the church (we note how his early education was paid for by the church), he moved gradually to another stance. One reason for the change was his continued contact with Christian humanists.

During his formative years Calvin also came into contact with certain men who were of Lutheran orientation. For example, while studying at Orleans and Bourges, the young man conversed with Melchior Wollmar, an ardent Lutheran, who showed him Luther's *Catechism* and the famous *Treatise on Christian Liberty.* Such exposure to the new winds helped drive the student farther along the path to reform.

It was not until sometime in 1533 that Calvin experienced what has been called his "conversion." Calvin described it simply as a turn to "docility and teachableness." He felt himself "seized by God and compelled to obedience." (This emphasis on obedience becomes a central point in his religious view as we shall see in a moment.) From this time the issues of religion were the central matters in his life, and he began a period of theological development that is nothing short of amazing. Within two years of this being "compelled to obedience" he had produced *The Institutes.* In later years he would bring out new editions in which the original material was added to and reworked, but in none of these is there a shift from the position of 1536. A mature and closely reasoned work had come from a young man of twenty-six.

Forced to flee from Paris before the persecution of Protestants led by King Francis, Calvin eventually came to rest in Geneva, a commercial city in western Switzerland. The Reformation had influenced the political situation in the city, and now, under the leadership of William Farel, an attempt was being made to bring some spiritual reality to the change as well. Farel prevailed upon the now-famous Calvin to stay and help him in this task. Their labors were short-lived, for after only two years (1536-38) the city fathers had had enough of the stringent measures advocated by the two, and removed them from their posts.

Upon the insistence of Martin Bucer, a leader of the Reformation in south Germany, Calvin joined him in Strassburg, where, for three years, he served a congregation made up of French Protestant refugees. These years were among the happiest of his life. He served as pastor, lectured on theology, married the woman who was to be a faithful companion until her death in 1549, and engaged in writing to further the cause of reform.

In the meantime the tide of opinion and power had changed in Geneva. A political revolution had taken place, and a party favorable to Calvin and his reforms was in control. In 1541 he was persuaded to return to the city where he lived until his death in 1564, struggling always to make it a Christian commonwealth according to his understanding of the Scriptures. The battle was long and arduous. At times the issue seemed in doubt, especially between 1549 and 1555, but in the end Calvin's indomitable will and personality carried the field. His impress upon the city and upon world Protestantism has lasted to this day.

The Call to Obedience

Calvin's theological stance is characterized by the fact that it is basically a compromise with other groups. The positions of Luther and Zwingli are both represented in the Genevan reformer. Zwingli's influence came by way of his successor at Zurich, Bullinger, who held a modified Zwinglian position; the contribution from Luther came mainly through men like Bucer and Melanchthon, Luther's co-worker in Saxony. The final stance was closer to Luther than Zwingli, but both strains are evident. Calvin took this material and also great pieces from the early theologians, especially Augustine, reworked the whole through his own understanding of the Bible, and produced a system that was to influence the whole of the Protestant world. His genius for systematic, logical clarity was of immeasurable significance for the Reformation.

By comparison Luther was an unsystematic, occasional writer, attacking particular problems as they appeared, with no apparent regard for order and design. His writings do show, however, a basic consistency, a steely core that unifies the whole. This core is his emphasis on the person and work of Christ.

While it is always dangerous to try to pick major themes for a person of such tremendous talent and voluminous writing, we will try to do so for the sake of comparison. If "trust" was the main concept, the key word, the essence of the Christian existence for Luther, one might say that for Calvin it was "obedience." This emphasis comes from his understanding of God.

It is of crucial importance for Calvin that one arrive at a knowledge of God. The greater part of the *Institutes* is devoted to this task. This knowledge involves far more than mere intellectual comprehension. It is not concerned with speculation but rather is directed toward Christian piety, which for Calvin is "that reverence joined with love of God which the knowledge of his benefits induces."[2]

One comes to a knowledge of the divine in two ways, both of which have been given by God. The universe itself speaks of its divine creator, and from it the listening man can learn of God. Such a source is not certain, however, because of the limitations of man. As a creature out of tune with God, i.e. as sinner, man's constant temptation is to take the news of God in the universe and pervert it into idolatrous worship.

The only sure way to knowledge of God, therefore, is in the Scriptures. It is in this place alone that one comes to see him as the one who redeems. Calvin's emphasis on the Scripture is due to the influence of Luther. This principle of understanding was an open turning away from the Roman Catholic position that Christian teaching was to be based on Scripture *and* tradition. Even the reformers were not willing to go all the way on this *Sola Scriptura* theme, however, and continued to emphasize the early creeds in addition to the Bible. Calvin held that the Bible contained all we need to know, now and in eternity, and that its authority is based on the activity of God himself. Scripture is the mirror in which God is seen, and from which we can learn his will and intention for us. It is only from this source that we can gain a true and saving knowledge of him.

The mercy of God and his forgiving nature in Christ are emphasized in Calvin as in Luther, but an additional facet is also developed that is characteristic of the French reformer. This facet presents the sovereignty, the majesty of God, in a fashion unequaled since the days of the prophets. Coupled with these themes is the understanding of God as divine legislator and lawgiver.

God is sovereign. He is the sole ruler of all. Everything depends upon him and his will. The "whole world is in his hands," to borrow a line from the spiritual, and not a bird falls from heaven, nor even a hair from one's head, but that God is involved. So also, in the religious realm, no one can come to God unless it is his will, and no one turns away, or remains in his evil unless the divine will is involved.

An important teaching of Calvin is related to the notion of divine sovereignty. Calvin wondered why some heard the promises and believed, while others, exposed to the same preaching, the same Word, continued in the old ways. He concluded that the two reactions were dependent upon God's will. He also was passionately concerned that no one make the mistake of claiming credit for the fact that he was living in the relationship of faith. This new life is due solely to the mercy and action, the will of God.

It was in this context that Calvin formulated the doctrine for which he is most widely known, that of predestination or election. Now, the Bible speaks of God predestining those of the household of faith (Rom. 8), i.e. God knows and holds those who believe. This is a promise of tremendous encouragement and comfort, for God is seen as holding fast to his own forever. Nothing can steal the believer out of the almighty hands. In the biblical presentation nothing is said about those who are outside of faith. Calvin, however, moving with logical precision, extends the notion of predestination to the condemned as he writes:

> Predestination we call the eternal decree of God by which he has determined with himself what he would have to become of every man. For . . . eternal life is foreordained for some and eternal damnation for others. Every man, therefore, being formed for one or the other of these ends, we say that he is predestinated to life or to death.[3]

This was, as he put it, "a horrible decree," yet he did not shrink from it. His concerns were to assert the divine sovereignty, to prevent any notion of merit, and to explain as far as possible why some believed and some rejected the promises. "My only object," he wrote, "is to subdue the pride of the human spirit, and to teach it to reverence, in all fear and humility, the majesty of God."[4]

Influenced perhaps by his own background in the study of law, Calvin sees this majestic, all-sovereign God as expressing himself as legislator and lawgiver in the Scriptures. This theme runs through all of his writings. God is the giver of law, who is to be obeyed. The Scriptures themselves find their inner unity in the divine will expressed in terms of legislation. The whole of Scripture is binding on the Christian in a much more rigid way than Luther, for example, would assert.

In view of this understanding of God which, while holding to the fact that he is benevolent Father and merciful, still emphasizes the sovereignty, majesty, and legislative aspects, how is the believer to respond?

Calvin held, with the earlier reformers, that God is absolutely trustworthy and that his promises in Christ are to be received in trust. The life of the believer is a life of trust. The Genevan reformer adds to this a theme that is characteristically his own: The life of the believer is also one of obedience. The almighty sovereign who speaks not only as benevolent father, but also as legislator, lawgiver, and judge, is to be obeyed. As Calvin puts it, "nothing is more acceptable to him than obedience."[5]

Calvin's attitude regarding obedience to God is clearly seen in the situation which first brought him to Geneva. Traveling as a refugee, he was trying to reach Strassburg where he hoped to live quietly and devote his life to academic pursuits, furthering, if possible, the Reformation by his pen rather than by personal combat. This fit his naturally shy and retiring nature. He was not the warrior type as was Luther. The main road was closed because of war, and the detour led through Geneva. There he was confronted by William Farel, the fiery reformer in Geneva, who desperately needed the help of the already-famous Calvin. He invited him to stay; Calvin refused, saying he felt called to serve by writing and that he was going on to Strassburg. At this point Farel thundered at him, "If you refuse to devote yourself with us to the work . . . God will condemn you."[6] The surprised and terrified Calvin felt that the Lord was calling him, and he could not disobey. Putting aside his earlier plans and his naturally diffident nature, he obeyed and became the reformer of Geneva, involved in bitter controversy nearly to the end of his days.

Though he emphasized obedience, at no time did Calvin allow anyone to rely upon his performance of the law as a means of salvation.

> For justification is withdrawn from works, not that no good works may be done, or that what is done may be denied to be good, but that we may not rely upon them, glory in them, or ascribe salvation to them.[7]

The theme of obedience runs through Calvin's whole treatment of the Christian life. He shares with Luther the understanding that the believer is at the same time a sinner and yet accepted by God in faith. Because of this he asserts that no one can rely upon the Law and works, since "We have not a single work going forth from the saints that if it be judged in itself deserves not shame as its just reward."[8] Nonetheless it is possible to prove, as it were, one's place among the elect by works. They can serve as a sign for the believer of his faith and election. As Calvin writes,

> Those who by true faith are righteous prove their
> righteousness by obedience and good works, not
> by a bare and imaginary mask of faith.[9]

His understanding of the church is also conditioned
by his concern for disciplined obedience. Calvin agreed
with Luther that the presence of the church could be
determined by the true preaching of the Word and
the proper administration of the Sacraments but added
a third mark, discipline. Even the structure of the
church has been determined by the Divine Legislator
and given in Scripture. To this form we must conform
and have pastors, teachers, deacons, and elders. Luther, in contrast, felt that the form of the church on
earth was subject to change and should be governed
by the needs of the time; whatever form contributed
best to the preaching of the Gospel should be used.

In short, the whole of the believer's life should re-
sound to the glory of his Creator and Redeemer. The
chief end of man is to give glory to God. We are to
do this because we are his and not our own. In a passage that beautifully summarizes all that we have
been trying to outline, Calvin writes:

> Now the great thing is this: we are consecrated
> and dedicated to God in order that we may there-
> after think, speak, meditate and do, nothing except
> to his glory. For a sacred thing may not be applied
> to profane uses without marked injury to him.
>
> If we, then, are not our own but the Lord's, it is
> clear what error we must flee, and whither we
> must direct all the acts of our life.
>
> We are not our own: let not our reason nor our
> will, therefore, sway our plans and deeds. We are
> not our own: let us therefore not set it as our goal

to seek what is expedient for us according to the flesh. We are not our own: in so far as we can, let us therefore forget ourselves and all that is ours.

Conversely, we are God's: let us therefore live for him and die for him. We are God's: let his wisdom and will therefore rule all our actions. We are God's: let all the parts of our life accordingly strive toward him as our only lawful goal. O, how much has that man profited who, having been taught that he is not his own, has taken away dominion and rule from his own reason that he may yield it to God.[10]

We are not our own, we are God's, and our highest worship of him is obedience. This, the basic understanding of Calvin, has also guided his spiritual descendants, down to our own day.

The reformer of Geneva took varied tunes from other composers of his time, some from Luther, a bit from Zwingli, much from Bucer, and blended them with his own biblical and patristic themes to produce a beautifully precise and logical melody. The order, harmony, and precision of his position were needed at that particular moment in the Reformation. A systematic planner had been needed, and provided.

Footnotes

[1] John Calvin, *Institutes of Christian Religion,* ed. J. T. McNeill, trans. F. L. Battles (Philadelphia: Westminster Press, 1960) II, 8, 5.

[2] Calvin, *Institutes,* I,2,1. McNeill-Battles edition, *op. cit.,* p. 41.

[3] *Ibid.,* III, 21, 5.

[4] Cited in J. T. McNeill *The History and Character of Calvinism* (New York: Oxford U. Press, 1952), p. 211.

[5] *Institutes,* II, 8, 5, p. 371.

[6] McNeill, *op. cit.,* p. 136.

[7] *Institutes,* III, 17, 1, p. 803.

[8] *Ibid.,* III, 14, 9, p. 777.

[9] *Ibid.,* III, 17, 12, p. 816.

[10] *Ibid.,* III, 7, 1. p. 690.

4.

Birds of the Storm
—The Evangelical Radicals

Then Jesus told his disciples, "If any man would come after me, let him deny himself and take up his cross and follow me" (Matt. 16:24).

Moreover, the gospel and its adherents are not to be protected by the sword, nor are they thus to protect themselves. . . . True Christian believers are sheep for the slaughter; they must be baptized in anguish and affliction, tribulation, persecution, suffering, and death; they must be tried with fire, and must reach the fatherland of eternal rest, not by killing their bodily, but by mortifying their spiritual, enemies.[1]

There were wide varieties of opinion in the sixteenth century as to what constituted reformation of the church. Luther, for all his new understanding of religion in the Pauline terms of personal relationship, was really very conservative in regard to outward practices. He retained many vestiges of the old ways whenever they did not conflict with the Gospel as he understood it. The basic order of service in the Lutheran areas, for example, did not differ in form from the older Catholic pattern. Calvin and Zwingli were not satisfied with this element in Luther and turned consciously to an effort to return to the patterns of the primitive church. They were much more radical in their efforts than the German.

Even these men, however, were conservative when compared to the genuine radicals of reform. It is to one such group that we turn in this brief chapter.

Some years ago it was customary to dump the so-called radicals into one big pot and condemn them all as either religiously heretical or politically seditious. This trend of interpretation was begun by Luther, Calvin, and Zwingli, and has been perpetuated to our day. In recent years, however, due mainly to the efforts of Mennonite scholars, a new look has been taken. Our generation is able to see various levels and types within the radical movements. Not all of them were of a revolutionary type.

The Counterpoint

Our concern is with that branch of the group which might be called the "evangelical radicals." Their history and understanding of religion provide an interesting counterpoint to the pictures already given.

In German-speaking Switzerland the leading reformer was Ulrich Zwingli. The headquarters for his activity was the town of Zurich, where the Reformation was established by vote of the council after a series of public debates in 1523 and 1524. Zwingli appeared to have won the battle over his conservative Catholic opponents when, in 1525, a new, radically simplified service was held in the great church in Zurich. All of his opponents, however, were not on the conservative side. As early as 1522 there had been a small group gathering regularly for Bible study. Its members felt that the reform of the church was going on at far too slow a pace. After the public debates in 1523 and 1524 they became convinced not only that Zwingli was moving too slowly, but that he was not even going to go on to real reformation at all.

One main point of contention was the understanding of the church. The radicals felt that the church should be made up of experiential Christians, i.e. those who were personally aware of and responsible for their faith and voluntary commitment to Christ. Zwingli, holding the more conservative view, maintained that all who were baptized, including infants, were members, and that membership in the church was also equivalent to citizenship in the state or commonwealth.

As a symbol of their dissatisfaction the radicals stopped presenting their children for baptism, maintaining that only conscious believers could be baptized. The city council, faced with this minor revolt, ordered that all infants in the city be baptized, and in reaction to this the radicals held their first *adult* baptism on January 21, 1525. The lines had now been drawn, and the battle was about to begin. Because the adult baptism of the original group was really a rebaptizing, since they had all been baptized as infants, their opponents called them Anabaptists, the name which has remained with them to this day.

Reaction to the radicals' action was not long in coming, nor was it tolerant in any sense. At first the authorities, both of church and state, did not really know what to do with these Christians, and there were public debates. Some were imprisoned, others hounded from the cities. The fact that they were actively persecuted in Zurich and other places led to a period of rapid expansion. Driven out of one city by ordinances against them, the members went to other places, and wherever they stopped they were active propagandists. They were without doubt the most aggressive missionaries of the entire period.

Within three years of the first rebaptism, all of the early Swiss leaders had either died or been martyred. In Catholic territories they were generally treated as heretics and burned, or sometimes drowned in a hideous parody of what their fault seemed to be. In Bavaria, Dukes William IV and Louis laid down the rule: "All Anabaptists are to be punished with death. Whoever recants will be beheaded; whoever does not recant will be burned."[2] In Protestant areas there were also reactions because of the religious deviation, but the Anabaptists were generally treated as seditionists because of their attitude toward the state and its responsibilities and powers. They were either killed or driven out as subversives. Some islands of toleration existed, such as Hesse in central Germany and parts of Moravia (modern Czechoslovakia), but the general treatment of the group is a terrible mark on the history of the church and on mankind in general.

Under persecution the teachings spread, first to

other parts of Switzerland, then to south Germany where Augsburg and Strassburg were important Anabaptist centers. Large groups went east to Moravia where the noble Lichtenstein brothers afforded a place of refuge on their estates. Another brand of the radical message went down the Rhine valley with figures like Melchior Hoffman who preached that the world was coming to an end and that the saints should establish the kingdom of God by force. Such rabid preaching actually caused a group of the most radical type to seize the city of Münster in northwest Germany in 1534-5, driving out both Catholic and other Protestant forces and setting up a commonwealth replete with polygamy and a form of communism. This aberration is an exception to the general position of the group as we will see in a moment.

Unfortunately for the moderates, the entire Anabaptist movement was identified with the Münster group, and so the Catholics and main-line Protestants felt absolutely justified in their programs of persecution. After the Münster catastrophe the quietistic groups again came into their own. Living in out-of-the-way areas, such as the Low Countries, they gathered together and perpetuated their ways and beliefs. Their descendants are still among us in the Mennonites and Hutterites.

The Call to Discipleship

At the risk of grave oversimplification, we have, in the last chapters, suggested that the central concept in religion for Luther was trust, and for Calvin, obedience. To follow the same general approach we can now assert that for the evangelical radicals the key was discipleship. With the other reformers these people talked about justification by faith, but they refused to stop there and went on to dwell on the new life that should follow justification. Their concern was the newness of character that resulted. The overriding interest in the ethical life, where love would be predominant, led them to be extremely critical of both contemporary Catholicism and Protestantism, for it seemed to them that in these camps there was a marked lack of newness of life and love. In all honesty, as we look at the bitter controversy that characterized the period, we must agree with the radicals' evaluation.

They emphasized, above all else, the idea of discipleship and its meaning.[3] The command to discipleship was, of course, found in the Scriptures. The Bible had the same central place for the Anabaptists as it did for the other Reformation groups. They differed markedly from Luther, however, in seeing even the New Testament as basically a book of law, and from both Luther and Calvin in the literalism with which they read the texts. This literal approach led to dire consequences in their relationship with society as a whole. When they claimed that as Christians they could not participate in government, bear arms, pay taxes, swear oaths, and the like, it seemed that they were bent on undermining the whole structure of society. This is the reason they were regarded as seditious in some Protestant areas. The whole position is based on a very literal understanding of the Gospels, especially the Sermon on the Mount.

While the early group emphasized the scriptural principle strongly, some came also to speak of an "inner light," by which a person could have revelations quite apart from the written Word. The major reformers reacted violently against this idea because of its complete subjectivism and because, without the check of Scripture, any form of activity may be said to be inspired of God. The excesses of the revolutionary group, supposedly following divine inspiration, showed the wisdom of this evaluation.

Their concept of discipleship centered upon a number of things. One was obedience to the Great Commission (Matt. 28:19). When our Lord said, "Go and make disciples," he meant it. The Anabaptists, in persecution or in times of peace, were tireless and effective evangelists. Their leaders were active, even aggressive, in the propagation of the new view. Some, for example, the Swiss Blaurock, would stand up in the middle of a Catholic service, interrupt the proceedings and demand the right to speak and present their views. Such demands could not help arousing considerable opposition.

The understanding of discipleship also centered on the ideas of love and non-resistance. These two themes were the controlling factors as the group faced inward and outward. Discipleship in terms of love and service was confined to existence within the committed community of believers. It was felt that such a group could exist without any serious involvement with the outer world of political power. Within this body the theme of love was to predominate.

The emphasis on love may be illustrated by reference to the community in Moravia that followed Jacob Hutter. Here the theme of brotherly love contributed to the formation of a society that practiced a type of Christian communism. Goods and wealth were shared, after the pattern of the New Testament congregation at Jerusalem (Acts 4:32 ff.). After all, if I love my neighbor as myself, how can I see him suffer for want of something which I have in abundance? Not all the radicals practiced this type of life, however, although it was generally charged that they did.

As the group faced the outside world, it practiced complete non-resistance. Since the use of the sword was, as they put it, "outside of the perfection of Christ," they avoided any involvement with force. This, of course, meant that they could not participate in the functions of government in any way. The main-line reformers had stressed the Christian's involvement *in* society, i.e. the working out of one's faith in the context of daily life. The radicals took the opposite tack, stressing that the believers live separated lives, avoiding entanglements with the political order. When contact did occur it would most often be in the form of persecution, and in this situation there could be no resistance at all, for conflict of this type was forbidden in Scripture.

Closely related to the practice of non-resistance and love was another point of emphasis in their understanding of discipleship. The disciple is one who is willing to suffer in the spirit of crossbearing. The church made up of such disciples is a suffering church; it bears the cross along with its Lord, and is willing even to be martyred. A critic might say that this understanding is merely making a religious virtue out of a historical fact, i.e. the group was suffering, and so they made this a part of their religious world-view. Whatever the cause, and part of it is most certainly their reading of the New Testament, it must be asserted that no group of this era was so willing to pay the ultimate cost of discipleship.

Another major thrust in their understanding of discipleship had to do with separation. The believer was to be separated from all that was common, so that he might live a life of holiness. This understanding also prevented them from active participation in the affairs of the secular community, and they tended whenever possible to set themselves off. The overall goal was to give reality to the spiritual life, and they felt that this could best be accomplished by separation.

The goal of discipleship with its attendant ideas of love, non-resistance, suffering, evangelistic fervor, and separation, was to become reality in the church. The evangelical radicals agreed with main-line Protestantism that the church is the communion of saints. They disagreed, however, on the generally accepted idea that the church on earth has within it both the righteous and the unrighteous. The older argument had looked to Christ's references to the weeds growing among the wheat (Matt. 13:24 ff.), and had understood this to refer to the fact that there would be hyprocrites among the believers until the end.

The radicals protested: The church is a voluntary communion of experiential Christians, i.e. those who have experienced the reality of faith and love in their hearts. It is, therefore, a pure church and not one stained by imperfections. This basic understanding made the group reject all "state" or "folk" church positions. There baptism into the church was also equivalent to citizenship in the secular community, and there was an intimate tie between church and secular order. Instead of this there was to be a complete separation between church and state, and in addition each congregation was to be an autonomous unit, calling its own leaders without interference from other bodies. All of the early leaders denied the power of the state in religious affairs and advocated toleration. In this they represented a minority position among Christians of the era.

What can we say in summary about this group?

First, we should be careful not to perpetuate the mistaken judgment of the reformers themselves that the Anabaptists were a revolutionary, heretical group set on overturning the established order. While it is true that a small minority actually followed this path at Münster, their action is in no way characteristic of the whole movement. The majority, with its insistence upon non-resistance and suffering, are in direct contrast to the radicals at Münster.

In the main they represent an attempt to return to the simplicity of the primitive church, based upon a literal, legal reading of the Scriptures. Not basically concerned with theological formulation, their emphasis was on the reality of discipleship in the Christian life. As simple, Bible-reading Christians they wished to lead separated lives and were willing to pay the price of their convictions. Some of their ideas have become part of the common heritage which is ours. The separation of church and state, the voluntary principle of church membership where one joins because it is his wish, and the emphasis on the congregational form of church government, are all part of this heritage.

Not understood in their own day, persecuted and tormented by both state and church, they are only now coming into the respect which is due them.

Footnotes

[1] Conrad Grebel, 1524 letter to Thomas Muntzer, in *Spiritual and Anabaptist* Writers, eds. G. Williams and A. Mergal (Philadelphia: Westminster Press, 1957), p. 80.

[2] H. Klassen, *Mennonite Quarterly Review*, XXXIII, No. 3 (July, 1959), p. 187.

[3] See J. L. Burkholder in *The Recovery of the Anabaptist Vision*, ed. G. F. Herschberger (Scottdale, Pa.: Herald Press, 1957), pp. 135 ff.

5.

The Storm Hits Rome
— The Counter-Reformation

. . Go out and compel them to come in (Luke 14:23).[1]

Even if my own father were a heretic, I would gather the wood to burn him.[2]

The initial reaction within Catholicism to the work of Luther was one of rather casual disinterest. No one replied immediately to the Ninety-five Theses on indulgences. When the news of the monk's activities did reach Rome, Pope Leo X felt it was merely a squabble between two of the religious orders. The main seller of indulgences had been a Dominican, while Luther was an Augustinian. The deep religious issues involved and the possibility for either genuine reform within the church or schism were not apparent to the pope.

As time passed, however, and Luther was not silenced by threat or excommunication, indeed, as other reformers stepped into the battle in other areas, the Catholic Church had to respond. Large areas of once-Catholic Europe had been swept away in the currents of the Reformation, and even staunchly Catholic countries like Italy and Spain had pockets of Protestant thought. It was in this context that Rome moved to self-reform. The demands of the centuries were now to be answered because of the outrage and violence of Luther, the cold and pristine logic of Calvin, and the ethical example of the Evangelical Radicals.

Piety and Papacy

The reform was of two parts, or on two levels: piety and papacy. Those in the church who rejected the Protestant approach, but still wished for a pattern of reform which might be workable, did not have far to look. The church in Spain had already passed through a period of reform and was a militant, tightly knit, and disciplined body. It had experienced centuries of fighting on the peninsula against the Moors, descendants of the Arab hordes that had invaded Europe by way of Spain in the eighth century. For hundreds of years an armed truce had continued, but in the period leading up to the sixteenth century an active campaign was initiated to drive the Moors out of the country. In conjunction with this there was a drive against all sorts of religious deviation, and the result was a church molded by the fires of the Inquisition and strong in its militant aggressiveness.

Two things had happened in Spain. One was the rise of a type of quietistic, mystical piety. The superficial and often superstitious piety of the late Middle Ages gave way to a renewal of the best of the religious life and understanding of the so-called high Middle Ages. The mystical experiences, deep piety, and emphasis on self-giving love associated with figures like Saint Teresa and Saint John of the Cross in Spain came to set the pattern for much that would happen outside of that country.

The second notable factor in the Spanish renewal was the rise of a renovated Scholasticism. The great structure of medieval Scholasticism had fallen into disrepute in many circles, under the attacks of men like Duns Scotus and William of Occam. Now, in Spain, at universities like Salamanca, the architectural theology that had supported the faith of the Middle Ages appeared again, refurbished and renewed. It would prove of great value in combating the Protestants.

The Spanish pattern was available; now what happened when it was applied? Since Italy was the heartland of Roman Catholicism, perhaps we should start there. Two parties came into being in reaction to the Protestant furor. On the one hand, the moderates (or progressives, to use a more modern term) were led by Cardinals Contarini and Sadoleto. They favored compromise with the Lutherans wherever possible and also a thoroughgoing reform of both clergy and papacy. The other reform wing was composed of the radicals (or conservatives) led by Bishop Caraffa who favored a return to the ideal of medieval purity and theology.

While the moderates and radicals were jockeying for position in the reform program, the papacy itself was undergoing changes, at least differences appeared in the men who occupied the papal throne. Of the earlier popes of the period only Adrian VI had grasped the significance of the new currents. He expressed himself as anxious to reform the church, but his reign was so brief that nothing was accomplished. His successor, Clement VII, was a typical Renaissance figure, not really a spiritual leader of the church, and not competent to deal with the conflicts in the north.

When Paul III became pope in 1534, the Counter-Reformation got under way. Though Paul was a Renaissance man in outlook, he did appoint a commission to study reform. Both Contarini and Caraffa were on this body. The conservative position carried the day. This victory was to set the tone for the whole movement for reform. During Paul's reign a number of extremely important things happened: The Jesuit order was confirmed; the Inquisition was reluctantly approved for use in the crisis; and in 1542 a church council was called which was to meet at Trent.

Paul's two successors were not significant in the reform of the church, but in 1555 a new pope was elected who took the name of Paul IV. Before his election he had been known as Giovanni Caraffa! The election of this dynamic conservative marks a real turning point in the history of Roman Catholicism. This strict, deeply pious, and strongly anti-Protestant figure turned gay, immoral, Renaissance Rome into a somber, ecclesiastical city. The popes from then on were mostly strict, strenuous Catholics. Catholic earnestness had been revived and along with it an intense opposition to the Protestant cause.

The Tools of Reform

As the Counter-Reformation began and continued its program, it became apparent that it had three major tools or arms: the Inquisition, the Jesuit Order, and the Council of Trent.

As early as the Fourth Lateran Council (1215) and the Synod of Toulouse (1226) the Inquisition had been established as an aid in the fight against heresy. Simply put, the Inquisition was a device to search out heresy and then to correct or destroy it. Hopefully, this could be done without force, but power, even torture, could be used. After all, it was reasoned, it is far better that one suffer for a short while now in order to be corrected, than to suffer eternally because of some false religious notion. While the very idea of an agency to pry out and, if necessary, destroy, deviant religious ideas is distasteful to modern thought, still it must be remembered that to the medieval church nothing was seen as being as dangerous or deadly as heresy. It was a far greater crime to lead a person into heresy than to murder him, for if he was only killed, his soul was still safe if he died in the faith; while if he had been led into false belief, he was lost forever. The church saw the discovery and, if possible, the conversion of deviants as part of its mission. The Inquisition is really a case of a pious

motive gone mad. It soon became a means by which
one's enemies could be eliminated and another's
property seized. How many innocents met death un-
justly will never be known.

In fifteenth-century Spain the Inquisition had been
used, under the government, not the pope, as a means
of cleansing the country of those who were thought
undesirable—the Jews and the Moors. In 1542 it was
introduced into Italy. Paul III was hesitant, but bowed
to the arguments of Bishop Caraffa, and in ten bloody
years Lutheranism in Italy was stamped out. Lutheran
interest had centered in Venice, Ferrara, and Naples,
and had never been a popular movement. The pattern
of suppression established in Italy was used wherever
the Catholic groups were strong enough to control
government and populace.

Of greater significance in the counter-reform movement was the Jesuit Order. In August of 1534 one of
the outstanding men of the century—nobleman, former soldier, student, pilgrim, Ignatius Loyola, gathered
a group of six friends around him in the Church of
St. Denis in Paris. They pledged themselves to go to
Jerusalem to do mission work, and if this plan were
blocked, they vowed to place themselves at the dis-
posal of the pope for any use that he desired. They
called themselves "the company of Jesus," and saw
themselves as a military order. They were not really
an order at this point, but only a student group with
strong anti-Lutheran and evangelistic feelings.

Their desire for foreign work was thwarted, and
the group turned to home mission work. In 1540 the

order was confirmed, and the papacy had acquired its strongest weapon in the battle against the new forces in the north. A vow of absolute obedience to the pope was required of all members, and indeed the concept of absolute, unquestioned obedience has long since been the heart and strength of this disciplined order.

Its main work became combating heresy. The Jesuits were the real shock troops of the Counter-Reformation. They also excelled in education and in the reform of church practice, where they insisted on regular preaching and on frequent confession as tools for the rejuvenation of piety. Some of the most famous Catholic missionaries come from this order. One of the original members of the group that met in Paris was Francis Xavier, one of the five or six greatest missionaries in the history of the church.

After a rather checkered career, including "suppression" in 1773 and renewal by Pius VII in 1814, the order continues to this day as one of the bulwarks of Catholicism. It has persevered in its educational emphasis and is the most powerful single order in the Catholic Church.

The third arm, or tool, of the Counter-Reformation was the Council of Trent. The church had remembered the days when councils had healed the schism of the fourteenth and fifteenth centuries, and calls for a council of reform had come from time to time during the fifteenth and sixteenth centuries. Luther, for example, had twice appealed to a general council for a decision in his case, and the Emperor, Charles V, in-

sisted that a meeting be held to heal the rift and reform the church. Initially the popes of the era were
hesitant about convening a council, for there was
always the possibility that such a body might declare
itself superior to the papacy. In 1542 Paul III finally
called for the convening of a council. It was to meet at
Trent, a city which was in German territory, though
south of the Alps, and thus virtually under papal
control.

The Council met intermittently for about twenty
years. Its course was a stormy one, and at one time
the delegates split, part going to Bologna, part remain-
ing at Trent. At another time, 1552, the group scattered
hurriedly when the news came that a Protestant army
was moving south. The Council fathers had no wish
to debate theology at sword's point.

The sessions themselves were also stormy, for many
factions were represented. Papal supporters found
themselves at odds with the adherents of the emperor, who persisted in the demands that the council
deal with reform in the church before doctrinal discussions. The Gallican party, which favored the idea
of semi-independent national churches, was opposed
by the so-called Ultramontanists (across the moun-
tains), who held that the proper form of church government was that one which was centered at Rome in
the person of the pope. The Franciscan and Dominican
orders argued over certain positions regarding the
Virgin Mary.

In every instance of controversy the papal position
won out, for the voting was controlled by Italian

bishops, and the decisions of the council had to be sanctioned by the pope.

We obviously cannot condense the meetings of twenty-odd years into a few paragraphs, but some significant decisions can be outlined. On the matter of Scripture and tradition, for example, it was asserted that the unwritten tradition of the church was authoritative and to be received on an equal basis with the Scripture. This decision widened and made permanent the gulf between Catholicism and Protestantism. In addition, it was asserted that only the Catholic Church has the right of interpretation of the Scripture, thus attempting to deny Protestants the basic documents of the faith.

On the matter of how a person comes into fellowship with God, the Council insisted that it was not to be seen as a declarative act of God by which the sinner is accounted righteous because of Christ, but rather as a subjective process in which one grows as he exercises his own powers and as he is assisted by the inpouring of grace. The grace of God, seen as an enabling power or substance, is emphasized; salvation is by God's grace, but room is left for the meritorious acts of man. Salvation is due to God's goodness, but man has to become fit as he uses his natural powers, aided by the Holy Spirit. One works, and thus merits an increase of grace. It is even possible to do more than is required for acceptance, i.e. to acquire more merits than are needed. This is known as supererogation.

Certain canons or rules for reform also came from

the Council. There was to be public instruction in the Scriptures, bishops were to preach, and the clergy to instruct the people. The very fact that such rules were needed speaks volumes about the condition of the church at the time. Seminaries were started in order to get the theological students away from the corrupting influence of the secular universities. Various moral regulations for the clergy were established, and an Index of books which the pious were not to read was also set up.

The Council, both in its theological and practical pronouncements, was basically a renewal of the medieval positions now formulated and finalized in opposition to the teachings of the Reformation. The great significance of Trent lies in its anti-Protestant stance and in the fact that its decrees are normative to this day.

Footnotes

[1] Passage used since days of Augustine to justify the use of force in bringing men into the church.

[2] Statement of Pope Paul IV (1555-59), a leader in the Counter-Reformation. Cited in Ludwig Pastor, *The History of the Popes, from the Close of the Middle Ages* (London: Kegan Paul, Trench, Trubner and Co., Ltd., 1924), Vol. XIV, p. 302.

6.

Does Reform Continue?

Not that I have already obtained this or am already perfect; but I press on to make it my own, because Christ Jesus has made me his own . . . one thing I do, forgetting what lies behind and straining forward to what lies ahead, I press on toward the goal for the prize of the upward call of God in Christ Jesus (Phil. 3:12-14).

Ecclesia reformata semper reformanda est: "The reformed church is always reforming."—motto of the Reformed Churches[1]

The Reformation is not only a particular movement at a moment in history. It is also an attitude that is willing constantly to reexamine the present and to use the insights of the past so that it may speak the biblical message to each new generation.

Two directly opposing views spring up when we ask if it is possible to have a Reformation today. There are those, for example, who insist there is no need for any sort of reform in the church, at least in their particular part of it, while others claim that the motto of the church in every age should be: "The church must always be reformed."

77

Should We Go On?

"Let's stop all this nonsensical talk about reforming the church—that took place in the sixteenth century." Many individuals feel this is the only proper answer to calls for reform. These say we have the truth of God's revelation of himself in the Scripture, and we have the correct interpretation and presentation of this truth in the confessions of our particular church body. What we need, therefore, is not reform, but a return to the solid bedrock upon which our fathers stood. We have the truth, and we have it properly stated.

If one has this basic position, then theological concern centers itself on repeating what has been said in the past. This is best done by using language that is also borrowed from other centuries. The attempt is made to reduce the truth of God into manageable formulae or statements, which are then to be mastered. The next step, communication, is accomplished by simply repeating what one has capsulized and memorized. This is a live option. Many Christians of both Catholic and Protestant persuasion are exercising themselves in this very course. If one accepts this stance, then it is correct to say that the church does not need to be reformed; it simply needs to return to its old statements and leaders, like Luther, Calvin, or perhaps, the Council of Trent.

Another group maintains that the church must always be in the process of reform. It must always be moving. This is true because of its very nature. The church is not a pile of bricks and steel standing on the corner of First and Main Streets, nor is it a great structure of congregations, conferences, and synods whose goal is the perpetuation of some ancient forms in a changing world. According to the New Testament the church is the *people* of God who are living in the newness and vitality of a relationship of faith with Jesus Christ. The church, again in New Testament terms, is a living organism, a body which has Christ as its head. Just as the body is in constant change, casting off and renewing, so the church, as body of Christ, has its being in change and renewal. It lives, moves, and changes to be able to serve and thus bring others into the same dynamic relationship. If we are willing to think of the church as a living body, headed by Christ, then we must also be willing at least to admit the *possibility* of change, reform, and renewal, for such change is of the essence of life itself.

Another reason for a concern for continual reform is to be found in the view of the Christian man held by the reformers themselves. Both Luther and Calvin insisted that the believer is at the very same moment both justified and sinner. That is, the marks and the weakening nature of sin are never apart from the believer in this life. What this means in our current discussion is that the formulators of the statements which we hold so dear were themselves finite beings, subject to error. There is always the possibility that our forefathers were as prone to one-sidedness and just plain stubbornness as we, their descendants, are.

There is, therefore, a great danger when we attempt to absolutize any theological system, whether it be

Lutheran, Anglican, or Catholic. We must always be aware that our words, our confessions of faith, cannot contain God nor take the place of our Lord and his self-disclosure. They are limited expressions, conditioned by their times and the prejudices of their writers. They must be constantly examined and reexamined lest they give the church a concrete rather than a dynamic character.

The church is also called to continual reexamination of its position by the challenges presented to it by other bodies and disciplines. This in no way means that the basic message is to be brought into conformity with the questioners, but rather that if we are to confront those with honest queries, we must be willing to listen to them and honestly attempt to answer what *they* are asking, not what we *wish* they were asking. We should not assume, for example, that the humanist, with his concern for man and his capabilities for progress, is not deadly serious in his quest for meaning and truth. The secularist, with his concern for the world and his disdain for anything that is not this-worldly, is also engaged in a search for reality. The questions he is asking are real and deserve to be answered. The existentialist, for whom life has content and meaning only in the decision of the individual, is also searching, looking for a meaning to life itself. These groups are posing problems of the utmost seriousness; they are asking questions which deserve answers. Whether or not the church can answer by simply restating the words of the sixteenth or some other century is a matter of real doubt.

The disciplines that fall within the bounds of natural science also present challenges to the church. The orderly, systematic study of the stuff of life and the accumulation of data based upon empirical studies and the principle of cause-effect seem to undermine the Christian view of God and the created order. Indeed they do challenge a certain understanding of God. To those, for example, whose whole faith is based on the premise that God has *dictated* the Scripture, word for word, the theories of natural science can seem demonic. To illustrate: a devout man, Archbishop Ussher, once calculated the date of creation by adding together the figures contained in the Old Testament. The year at which he arrived was 4,004 B.C. Now a certain type of Christian came to equate this type of calculation with the *heart* of the Christian message. After all, had not God dictated the numbers?

What was such a person to do (and what is he to do today) when the geologist points to the strata in a cliff and says it shows not 4,000 but 10,000 years of history? What is to be done when the archeologist sifts dust in a New Mexican cave and finds the remains of a race of hunters 25,000 years old? What can one say to the British anthropologist who discovered manlike remains in an African gorge that are from nearly 2,000,000 years ago?

The uneasy religious atmosphere of our century resulted, in part, from this type of confrontation and the naive insistence that one must choose either the Christian faith as identified with the dictation theory of Scripture, or the scientific answers. And the question remains: What is the church, the living body of Christ, to answer to these questions? Must it relegate all such inquiry to demonic influence, or can it openly face the honest problems of the modern world?

The church is also challenged by the fact that it lives in a period that is different from past eras, and that the situations in which it finds itself are also different. Luther never envisioned the power of a totalitarian state that aims at control of even a man's mind when he penned his now famous statements regarding obedience to the secular powers because they are established of God. Nor did the leaders of the sixteenth century have the slightest notion of the complexity of the modern industrialized age, complete with the problems of automation and leisure time. What type of challenge do these new problems and situations raise for the church? Is it possible that we must try to reaffirm the age-old message of man's relationship to God, broken by sin and reestablished in faith, to reaffirm this message in ways that do not fit the patterns set by our fathers?

Our call is to witness in *this century*, not the second, the sixteenth, or even the nineteenth. Our world is in ferment. Even to attempt to work honestly and responsibly in such an age, we must first of all stop living in the past, and then continually attempt to renew the church that it may speak as powerfully to our day as it did to Luther's and Calvin's. To do this, the church must always be reformed.

It obviously does no good at all simply to claim over and over that times have changed. What can be said to describe the religious character of our world? It is an age of ecumenical concern. It is part of the so-called "Post-Christian Era." It is a time of a continuing and passionate religious quest.

An Age of Ecumenical Concern

There is no doubt that while the religious upheaval of the sixteenth century brought about a new understanding of religion, it also caused great unrest and animosity within historic Christian bodies. There were some conciliatory figures on both sides who engaged in a whole series of discussions which ended in 1541. These men aimed at concessions and reconciliation, but were doomed to failure by the great depth of the split and by the intransigence of the dominant parties on both sides. The Protestant position became more and more set in opposition to Catholicism, and, in the Council of Trent, the same action took place in Catholicism. The lines had been drawn with great force and clarity.

A period of great bitterness followed. Catholics were outraged that the unity of Catholic Europe had been disturbed and the faith, as they understood it, perverted. Protestants were embittered by the charges that they were now "outside" the church, and by the means used to force them back into the fold. These "means" included a reinstated inquisition and the work of the Jesuits. A whole series of wars tore apart the European countryside as the religious issues were made a part of national schemes and ambitions.

Charles V, the emperor, moved against the Protestant princes to force them to comply with his religious wishes; they resisted. The French Protestants engaged in no less than eight wars to preserve their freedom. The Netherlands area was the scene of a long and bloody conflict which pitted Spanish Catholics against Protestant nationalists. In the seventeenth century the terrible Thirty Years' War devastated much of central Europe as conflicting armies marched back and forth, living off the land, plundering friend and foe alike.

The Protestant-Catholic animosity was increased by the persecutions carried on by zealots in each camp. Much has been written about the excesses of each party. It should be noted at this point, however, that neither side comes out of this picture with a clean report. There were instances of aggravated persecution on both sides. Protestants were burned in Catholic Spain and Italy, in the Netherlands, and under the brief rule of Mary in England; Catholics met similar fates during the reign of Elizabeth in England. Both Catholic and main-line Protestants sometimes treated the left wing of the Reformation with extreme cruelty. This was simply not an age of religious toleration and freedom.

The problems have, of course, continued right into modern times. They have been acute in areas of mission competition, e.g. in South America, and in places where one group has been in the minority. Protestants in predominantly Roman Catholic areas such as Spain have sometimes been subjected to many sorts of persecution, some subtle, others cruelly overt. Catholics have suffered the same fate at times, and Protestants should remember this, lest they become insufferably self-righteous. As late as 1844 there were anti-Catholic riots in Philadelphia in which thirteen persons were killed, fifty badly hurt. Two churches, a seminary, and blocks of houses were destroyed during this same episode that scars the history of a great city and country dedicated to freedom. More recently the activity of the Ku Klux Klan and the bitter anti-Catholic movement in American politics in 1924, 1928, and 1960 add further color to an already dark picture.

The divisions were not limited to those between Catholic and Protestant. Almost from the start there had been differences of opinion and interpretation between the reforming parties. Some, for example, wished to reform the church as rapidly and as completely as possible; others held that a conservative stance was best, and that only those things which were contrary to the Gospel should be removed. Points of emphases also varied. These differences were in some instances increased by the personalities involved. The theological differences of Luther and Zwingli, for example, were accentuated by personal animosity.

As the years passed, the divisions became firmly set along creedal lines. Even within creedal groupings there were different levels or emphases which depended on matters like geography, language, and social structure. The fact that there were, and are, Lutherans in the United States who still find it difficult to converse with each other, even though they share a common confessional stance, illustrates this admirably (or rather, unhappily).

In spite or perhaps because of this splintered picture of the church, some people began to wonder about the possibility of the oneness in Christ of which the New Testament speaks. This concern led to the period in which we live, an era marked by a coming together of Christian groups for mutual study and work rather than a further splintering. This type of coming together characterizes our age. It is called the Ecumenical Movement.

The seeds of ecumenical concern already were being planted in the eighteenth and nineteenth centuries. Several special areas of interest led to an exploration of possible ways of cooperation. One concern was for the mission outreach of the church. The scandal of Christian groups bitterly competing on mission fields when the great mass of pagans were waiting for the real work to begin was not ignored by some mission leaders.

Interest in work among students and Christian education in general also drove some to examine the possibility of common action. Societies for mission work that crossed the earlier strict denominational lines were organized, as were Bible societies. Those concerned with work among young people assisted in the formation of the Young Men's Christian Association in 1844.

In 1910 a World Mission Conference met in Scotland. This meeting was to prove a breakthrough in ecumenical relations, for it stepped beyond the in-

formal actions of earlier years and had official delegates who engaged in lengthy preliminary studies of
the problems and who had definite plans to imple-
ment the decisions made by the conference.

Other groups gathered to discuss various problems.
A council to study the Christian life and ethic was
organized and met in Stockholm, Sweden (1925), and
later in Oxford, England (1937). Another concerned
itself with the various expressions of the faith and
order, and met in Lausanne, Switzerland (1927), and
later in Edinburgh, Scotland (1937).

In 1938 at a meeting in Utrecht, Holland, a consti-
tution was drawn up for a new group that combined
two earlier bodies: the Council on Faith and Order,
and the Council for Life and Work. This new body,
meeting officially for the first time in 1948 in Amsterdam, was called the World Council of Churches and
described itself as "a fellowship of churches which
accept our Lord Jesus Christ as God and Saviour." It
had no legislative power over its members and was
simply a fellowship of autonomous churches which
aimed at facilitating common study, mutual understanding, and common action wherever possible.
Meetings of this body have been held at Amsterdam,
Holland (1948), Evanston, U.S.A. (1954), and New
Delhi, India (1961). It has its headquarters in Geneva,
Switzerland. Its membership includes the majority of
major Protestant bodies in the Americas, Europe, Brit-
ain, Australia, and Asia, most of the larger "younger
churches" in Asia and Africa, and nearly all Orthodox
and old Catholic Churches.

The coming together process has not been limited to groups of different confessional background. The major denominations have also found themselves involved and have founded cooperative bodies within their own borders. Presbyterians, Methodists, Baptists, and Anglicans, to name a few, have all moved in this direction. The Lutherans have also been moving. In 1923 the Lutheran World Convention was founded, and in 1947 the Lutheran World Federation. This is a federation of nearly all Lutheran bodies throughout the world, and has as its aim cooperative activity in missions, service, and theological research. In the United States the National Lutheran Council led in the same type of work on the national level. A new cooperative agency has been proposed to take the place of the NLC. It will be called the Lutheran Council in the United States of America (LCUSA), and will begin operations in January of 1967.

The increasing number of mergers within denominations is but another part of the ecumenical surge in our day. The situation within American Lutheranism illustrates the point. In the past five years mergers have taken place that helped erase the old ethnic and linguistic divisions of the immigrant period of Lutheranism in this country. At present there are three major Lutheran bodies here, The Lutheran Church in America (LCA), The Lutheran Church—Missouri Synod, and The American Lutheran Church (ALC). There is some hope that there may be further consolidation.

These attempts within Protestantism do not aim at the establishment of some sort of "super church."

While there are a few individuals who think in these terms, the documents of the World Council of Churches and the majority of its member churches have no such understanding. To continue to insist that this is the goal of all ecumenical groupings is to set up a straw man upon which one may then beat with little fear of counterattack. The creation of such a super church is not possible; the member bodies would not allow it.

The overall aim of the ecumenical endeavor has been the furtherance of common goals such as missions and service, the creation of a united front on some issues so that a greater impact may be made on the world, and the demonstration that there is indeed a "oneness" in Christ found among Christians.

The relationship of Catholicism to the ecumenical movements presents an interesting study in itself. As we noted earlier, the official attempts at dialogue ended in 1541, and in 1543 the Council of Trent assumed a rigid anti-Protestant stance. This movement by reaction continued to characterize Catholic development right up into the modern period.

As it faced and felt the new currents of ecumenical interest, Rome first responded by ignoring the new tide. There then followed a period of antagonism. Pope Pius XI condemned the ecumenical movement in 1928. It should be noted that the antagonism was mutual, e.g. the International Mission Conference had spoken out "against popery and superstition."

Gradually, however, a new spirit began appearing in Catholicism. Leo XIII (1878-1903) called Protestants "most beloved brethren," not heretics, schismatics, or sectarians, the language of an earlier age. Continued gains in regard to openness between Protestant and Catholic were made under Pius XII who spoke out for toleration of Christian minorities, a new lay emphasis in Catholicism, and Bible study. The movement dedicated to a renewal of the liturgy in the church began and gathered speed. Its goal was the Mass (communion service) in the language of the people, not in the Latin of the church.

The greatest impulse to active participation in ecumenical discussion came in the person of Pope John XXIII. Elected in October of 1958, at seventy-eight, the new pope was plainly thought of as an interim figure who would simply hold the line; he was to represent a resting place between more active rulers of the church. He fooled everyone in this. An active, warm, and very human person, John was deeply concerned with the problems of Christian unity, and in January, 1959, he called for a council of the Catholic Church to meet. This council was to concern itself with the growth of the Catholic faith, restoration of sound morals, and the adaptation of church discipline to the needs and conditions of the time. One thing that stands out about this call was its non-polemical nature. This gathering was not to be directed against anyone. "The council is rather intended much more to attract those who are outside the church than to condemn them."[2]

Some basic trends became evident in the deliberations of the council. There was, for example, criticism of the overcentralization in the Catholic Church and an insistence that both local bishops and laity be given more authority and responsibility. The long-standing relationship between the church and secular power and the accompanying temptation to use power were attacked, as were the extremes of ceremonialism and the unintelligible nature of the Mass. Also criticized, and this is very significant, was the anti-ecumenical mood that had prevailed since the Councils of Trent (1543-63) and Vatican I (1870).

Pope John died, and a new leader, Paul VI, took the throne. He reconvened the council and stated that among the aims of the council fathers should be the reform of the church. This use of the word "reform" was virtually unprecedented within Catholicism. Even Pope John had only spoken of "bringing the church up to date," and of "renewal," but now Paul had called for "reform." The church, he maintained, had not been substantially unfaithful to its divine founder, "but the council should seek to strip away what may be unworthy or defective in the church's tradition. . . . The church must be conformed to the living Christ."

The significance of the council for Catholics lies in the fact that it marks an official entry into the ecumenical discussion. The effects of such confrontation are already apparent in the new biblical emphasis, the insistence upon the Word and its preaching, and in other ways. It is also noteworthy as an attempt to make the Catholic Church speak to the modern world. How this concern and the attendant decisions will affect the local Catholic parish remains to be seen, but a great stride has been taken. Not even the conservative wing of Catholicism, which centers in the Curia, the bureaucratic body around the pope, can reverse the tide.

Protestants are also challenged by the Catholic entry into the modern ecumenical world. We are called upon to speak to the modern world and to study today's Catholicism so that we are aware of what is going on now, and thus no longer be content to merely repeat the stereotypes of the past. Above all, we are drawn to continual self-examination.

This great surge and movement in both Protestantism and Catholicism are all a part of the ecumenical age in which we live. There is no prospect of outward unity, but there is a chance that we may come to recognize our essential oneness as brothers in Christ, whether we are Catholic or Protestant. This is a great day for the church, for the community of believers. The era of polemics and clenched fists is past. Now there is at least a halting attempt at love and mutual understanding.

The Post-Christian Era

The age in which we live is part of what some call the "Post-Christian Era."

"Post-Christian Era"? Does this mean that we live in a time after true Christians have ceased to exist, a time in which faith is no longer a possibility? This phrase does not mean that it is too late now for Christianity, or that it is no longer around. It refers to something else. Its point of reference is the society that is *determined* by its Christian heritage and *formed* by its Christian content. There was a time when society and culture were indeed formed by Christianity. This period seems now to have passed.

The first three hundred years of the church were marked by sporadic persecutions. The old ways would not simply bow to the new, and the conflict was often marked by Christian blood. In the fourth century, however, an entirely new situation presented itself as the Emperor, Constantine, made the Christian faith the favored religion of the empire. In effect he made it the official faith. What a change: The days of persecution and conflict, the paths of martyrdom, all were in the past. The roles had been reversed; the persecuted were now the protected and favored, and the Christian community found itself and its destiny inextricably entwined with that of the empire.

Some hundreds of years passed, and by the time of the Middle Ages this intimate relationship had extended to all levels of life. The Western world was called the *Corpus Christianum,* "the Christian body," as the church became the dominant power in men's thinking.

Church and state were so closely tied that a pope like Innocent III in the thirteenth century could literally rule all of Europe, making and deposing kings as he chose. The church and education were linked in such a way as to make theology the queen of the sciences and all other studies subservient to it. God was sought in the rational exercises of the scholastics,

as well as in the piety of the cloister and the cere-
mony of the Mass. The structure of the church—its
secular, moral, intellectual, even scientific authority—
seemed unshakable. But cracks began appearing in
this authoritarian wall.

The power of the church in secular affairs was
challenged by a Dante and a Marsilius of Padua. The
intellectual structure of Scholasticism was cracked by
Duns Scotus and William of Occam, and the morality
and piety of the church, especially at its upper levels,
were scrutinized and found wanting by a Wyclif, a
Hus, and a Savonarola. The reformers and the movements of the sixteenth century contributed further to
the breakup.

And now we make another great leap—from the
sixteenth to the twentieth century. Four hundred years
have passed, and we find another new situation. The
Corpus Christianum, rooted in Constantine and flow-
ering in the Middle Ages, has withered and died. The
picture of a society molded and controlled by the
church has been replaced by a many-sided pluralism.
"There now exist social, political, religious and cultural pluralisms that are compounded by images and
habits of thought no longer effectively shaped by
Christianity."[3] In short, Christianity has lost its position
of automatic, privileged supremacy and must now
compete for the allegiance of men in the arena of
conflicting ideologies. There is no longer a Christian
culture, i.e. one that is formed decisively by Christian
teaching. No matter how much we try to convince
ourselves to the contrary by putting religious slogans

on coins or in official statements, the society of the world is definitely post-Christian.

Another problem is closely related. It deals with man's changed awareness or sense of God. If we look back to earliest years of the Christian tradition, we find a culture that was permeated with an awareness of the divine. The pagan world engaged in a religious quest through ancient or modern rites designed to placate or please the members of its pantheon. Shrines to Osiris, Dionysius, Venus, Diana, the Divine Emperor, and a host of others dotted the countryside and crowded the towns.

The Christian community also had its sense of God. Its confession was that "in the beginning God," and that now and throughout history man achieves real meaning only in relation to him and his work. As St. Augustine (d. 430) once put it, "Thou hast formed us for Thyself, O Lord, and our hearts are restless until they find their rest in Thee."[4]

The systems, pagan and Christian, existed side by side, each with its sense of the divine, and each claiming priority for itself. They competed for the allegiance of the world, and though the Christian community often found itself bathed in its own blood by persecution, it survived and grew.

Constantine's change in policy, mentioned earlier, did not affect this awareness of God. Throughout the Middle Ages one of the "givens" of life was that God existed and was concerned with his creation. The reformers of the sixteenth century continued in this tradition. Everything for them was oriented in relation to God, his purpose, his concern, and his action. The world and the church may tumble and vanish into chaos, but "God is from everlasting to everlasting," and he has spoken through the historical figure, Jesus the Christ, and wills to be present today.

As we look to our own day, we see something different. Ours is an age in which the traditional understanding of God is being questioned. Much of modern literature is based upon the premise that God, seen in the traditional way, is dead, that is, God is either irrelevant or non-existent.

Two related questions present themselves: How did this shift from the seeming solidity of the *Corpus Christianum* to the many-faceted pluralism of the twentieth century take place? And how can so many moderns live as though God were irrelevant or non-existent?

Many streams have combined to form this new attitude. There has been, for example, a change in the philosophical framework with which the modern world works. To illustrate briefly: The philosopher who is an empiricist emphasizes the data of sense perception and holds, in its extreme forms, that only that which can be tested or proved by the senses is of value. This concentration on "this world" led inevitably to a denial of whatever is transcendent, or beyond the realm of the senses.

Existentialism, another modern alternative, turned away from problems of God and essence to the issues of this life, i.e. of existence. Its most ardent proponents have often divorced themselves from any sense of, and search for, God in order to dwell continually on man and his problems. "There is no God," proclaims Sartre, no moral absolutes, and no significance in a life that becomes tolerable only in decisive action.

A different historical sense and study also contributed to the change in atmosphere. The problem posed by this new approach is plainly evident in the realm of biblical studies where scholars began applying the same tests to the biblical books regarding authorship, historical context, and meaning as they did to other works of the ancient world. What they discovered was exciting to some, leading to a whole new appreciation of God's work *in* history. The studies were destructive to the faith of others who became so enamored of the historical process that the workings of God in and through that process were forgotten or denied.

Another contribution to the change in atmosphere came from the study of natural science. The laboratory concern for proximate causes led some to a lack of interest in even the possibility of an ultimate cause; and the observation and recording of empirical data led to an attitude of disinterest regarding those things which could not be proved in this way. It seemed that science could indeed answer all man's questions, at least all those that had any relevance. The world had "come of age," to borrow Bonhoeffer's phrase, and did not need the notion of God to make sense of things as they were.

An Age of Religious Quest

Man by his very nature is engaged in a search, in a religious quest, for a principle of understanding by which meaning can be measured. In the absence of the structure of the *Corpus Christianum* upon which he could rely and of the sense of God that characterized earlier ages, he turned to other answers. He looked to other sources for the meaning of his life.

Some turned to materialism. The point of life was to be seen in terms of material gain. Wealth, prestige, and power were the answers to the riddle of existence. Man was seen as essentially an acquisitive animal, satisfied only in the acquiring of material wealth.

To others humanism was the answer. The apparent absence of anything that transcends humanity led to an assertion of man as the measure of all things. Coupled with this was an easy optimism about human capabilities. Given enough time and education, it was assumed that all the ills of the planet would disappear as the human race evolved.

To others, Marxism seemed an answer. This view combined the Hegelian dialectic with a materialism, mixed in a deep antagonism to the traditional religious concepts, and produced a program of revolution which was supposed to eventuate in a classless society where the ancient ills of man would not exist.

The search for a principle of meaning in a secular, pluralistic world has provided other answers of course. For example, nationalism, not only in newly-freed areas, but also throughout the world, appeared as the key. Scientism, the understanding that the meaning, significance, and hope for mankind is to come ultimately from the laboratory and library, appealed to others. When we discover enough, the golden age will be here.

The search goes on; answers are given on every hand. But each of the alternatives has shown itself to be less satisfying than at the first blush of enthusiasm. Certain questions continue to be asked:

Is man only an animal, who can be satisfied only with the accumulation of things?

Has Marxism done what it proposed to do, and thus proved itself to be the answer?

Has nationalism or supernationalism solved or created problems?

Is science the answer to the search for meaning? Have we advanced toward peace or only toward more effective means of war?

In short, is man the measure of all things; can the religion of self, whatever its name, provide ultimate meaning for life?

The religious quest continues. The inadequacies of the modern answers have caused a new concern for and interest in the Christian answer. The problem is: Can this Christian answer speak to the modern world, or does it really belong only to the childhood of humanity? If there is to be a confrontation between Christ and the modern world, if the church has the answer for the continuing search of man, then there must be a continuing reformation so that this message may be heard.

Footnotes

[1] Cited in J. C. McLelland, *The Reformation and Its Significance Today* (Philadelphia: Westminster Press, 1962), p. 109.

[2] Statement of Cardinal Tardini, quoted in *The Papal Council and the Gospel,* ed. K. E. Skydsgaard (Minneapolis: Augsburg Publishing House, 1961), p. 107.

[3] Paul Lehmann, "Protestantism in a Post-Christian World," *"Christianity and Crisis,* XXII, No. 1 (1962), p. 7.

[4] Augustine, *Confessions,* 1, 1, 1.

7.

Our Concern for Our World

For God so loved the world that he gave his only son, that whoever believes in him should not perish but have eternal life (John 3:16).

Hence, since everything we possess, and everything in heaven and on earth besides, is daily given and sustained by God, it inevitably follows that we are in duty bound to love, praise, and thank him without ceasing, and, in short, to devote all these things to his service, as he has required and enjoined in the Ten Commandments.[1]

The church must be in a continual process of reforming itself. This is true because of its very nature as a living, dynamic body, because of the finitude of the formulators of our dogmatic statements, however great they may be, because of the challenges of other bodies and disciplines to examine and reevaluate our positions, and because of the demands of our century. The ecumenical surge, the fact of Post-Christian existence, and the never ending quest for a principle of meaning in life all make such a reformation a requirement in our age.

Just as the only interpretation of the great events of the sixteenth century that gives an adequate picture is the religious one, since the efforts of the reformers were essentially directed toward the problems of relationship with God, so also our efforts must concentrate upon the same area. Our concern is that the message of Christ reach the world.

I am frankly and unashamedly Christian

I believe, not only that God is, but that he has been and *is active* in history. I believe that God has created and sustains the universe. I am *not* basically concerned, nor do I believe Scripture is, with *how* this was accomplished, nor with insisting that our age accept the world view of the first century.

I believe that man is God's creation and that as God's creature he needs more than food, warmth, power, and family; he needs life lived in relationship to God, the source of his being, the ultimate reality.

I believe that man is unable to achieve this relationship by himself; in fact, when left alone his most ardent searching results only in an increase of alienation with his fellows and within himself as pride places itself upon the throne.

I believe that God, who has been active in history in many ways, has come and reveals himself and his purpose in the person of Jesus Christ, and that all his promises of new life, of forgiveness, and meaning find their "yes" in him.

And I believe that God acts and speaks today, through his Word and the community of the faithful gathered about it, and that he also rules through the structures such as the home, education, and government, which the world calls "secular." Not that his actions in this realm are always perceivable, but he acts here nonetheless.

Now, these themes have always been offensive. Back in the first century Paul wrote that the Gospel, i.e. the news of God's activity in Christ, was "a stumbling-block to Jews and folly to Gentiles" (1 Cor. 1:23). And it is a place of stumbling and apparent foolishness today.

The very idea of sin and of my absolute dependence upon another offends my pride and sense of independence.

The particularity of the whole scheme, the use of a particular people ("How odd of God to choose the Jews"[2]), of a particular man, of a particular way to fellowship—all this challenges my hope that all might be acceptable, my desire for alternate routes, and independent action.

The affront is real and cannot be explained away without removing the heart of the Christian message. But this word, complete with its offensiveness, is the answer to the searching of our age. The problem of the church is to make this message relevant to our post-Christian, secular age; to use the wealth of the past together with the insights of the present in order to hold up Christ as the answer to the religious quest of our century, and of all of history. We are not allowed the luxury of retreating to the past, to the "good old days." *This* is our age, the time of our challenge. We must bring the Christian answer, good news and offense, in relevant fashion and not allow peripheral issues to cloud God's quest for us.

How can those of us who are committed to this answer do this? How can we move to reform, to "bring the church up to date," to use the words of the late Pope John XXIII? May I suggest some basic courses of action?

New Language

First: we must use the language of today.

This is not the first century, nor is it the sixteenth. We add to the offense of the Gospel when we insist on presenting it in ancient dress. For example, the biblical writers, inspired by God to present his Word, his answer, wrote against the background of *their* view of the world. Their ideas of science, e.g. of geography, are not essential to the Christian answer; they are not relevant; in some instances they are not even correct. Why should we continue to insist that the earth is the center of the universe, that the world is flat, that the heavens are held up by pillars and that above them is water? These elements of a world-view long since dead need not color our message today.

This means a scrapping of the view that God dictated the Scriptures; it means a return to the understanding that he conveys his message through human means and human limitations. This means recognizing that various types of knowledge come in different ways. The position that holds that the Bible contains all we need to know, now and in eternity, *is just not true*. When our children have measles or appendicitis, we go, not to the Bible, but to a doctor. Conversely, when concerned with the ultimate significance of death, as Christians we go, not to the autopsy rooms, but to the Scriptures, to the promises of God.

It is not only in world-view that Christians are sometimes centuries tardy, but also in words. Certain terms and themes are not really meaningful today. Only a small segment of the population has any real notion of what the words sheep and shepherd might mean when used to describe the believer and the Lord. Images that were pregnant with meaning in the day when they were first used do not speak clearly to another age. One task of the church is to translate into modern idiom the *content* of the message. For example, a city boy, having grown up on the streets of a metropolis without any knowledge of the country and its ways, once was asked to write his version of the Twenty-third Psalm. Instead of beginning, "The Lord is my shepherd," he wrote, "The Lord is my parole officer. . . ." The officer watching over the lad, guiding him and keeping him out of trouble, seemed the best image of the shepherd to this young man. Does this language offend us? It should not.

In the same vein, how about this for a prayer?

> My radio is on and, yes I'm listening to the news again. In a few minutes there'll be some more music.
>
> I want to get home, Lord, but the traffic won't move. I'm tired from working, tired of waiting, tired of listening to the stupid radio. I'm too damned tired to be patient, and I'm hot and sweaty. I've worked hard all day, and I want to get home. I don't feel like being loving or patient or kind or long-suffering. Not right now. Later, maybe.

If I could have anything in the world right now, it would be a road stretching out ahead, empty, all other cars gone, and a beautiful freeway for miles and miles, just for me, and then home. I've just about had it today. Really, it's too much. Don't ask me to be patient.

Okay, I'll try some more to be human, but it's nearly been knocked out of me for one day. Stay with me; I can't do it alone.

Jesus, thanks for sweating it out with me out here on this highway.[3]

A concern for contemporary language should also extend to our liturgies—the way the church worships. The churches of the Reformation heritage must also be willing constantly to reexamine this facet of their life together. Does our worship life speak today or do our churches seem to be merely museums for out-of-date ideas and artifacts? Do our clergy confront and challenge the world with the presence of the living Christ, or do they seem to be merely curators of a forgotten age?

There are signs of genuine renewal in liturgy in some quarters. The Catholic Church has its liturgical movement which strives for simplicity and the use of the common languages of the people rather than Latin. For some Protestants there is also a concern for both new forms and reexamined old ones that may better serve the common worship life. There is a willingness to experiment and even to fail if need be, in order to find meaningful means of expression. Others, however, see renewal only in terms of a return to the practice of the Middle Ages, and so they reintroduce vestments and practices uncommon for hundreds of years. It is ironic that at the precise moment when Rome is moving toward simplicity, some of us are going in the other direction. We may one day pass each other, like ships in the night!

There is a richness in the past which must not be lost. There is also a challenge in the present which must be met. A practice is not *necessarily* desirable simply because it is old, nor, however, is it *automatically* good simply because it is new. We must strive to use the best of both past and present.

Many of the great hymn tunes of the past came directly from the secular world. They were the popular melodies of the day, adapted for use in the service. Today similar experiments are being conducted. England has produced a Folk Mass, the service in modern dress. Comparable services, with jazz as the basic ingredient, have appeared in America. Just this year the great jazz musician, Duke Ellington, played a concert of sacred modern music in the Fifth Avenue Presbyterian Church in New York. Drums, cymbals, horns, and even tap dancing were used. Those who object too strenuously should read some of the Psalms again (Psalm 150 and others).

These efforts certainly grate on ears tuned to traditional ways, but they are expressive of love and devotion in contemporary form. We must be open to the possibility of their use and encourage the experiment. Our attitude should be one of joyful and hopeful experimentation. When we can face the use of new idiom in the church with, "Let's try it," instead of "No, it hasn't been done this way before," we will be at least on the way to speaking to our world.

New Questions

Second: we must seek to answer the questions of today.

The basic theme remains the same: man, alienated from God, can be complete only in relationship through Christ. But each age creates new variations and asks the old question in new ways. If the church persists in living in the past, it will find itself talking alone, i.e. to itself.

I sometimes have the disturbing feeling that the church is answering questions that most people are no longer asking. This is, for example, no longer the age of the bow and arrow, nor even of the high-powered rifle. What have we to say to a world quivering beneath the shadow of a mushroom-shaped cloud? Faced by the probability of total destruction should either side make an error, is it possible that we should be rethinking the reformers' positive assurances about the Christian supporting the "just war"? The world is just not as simple as it once was, and simple answers, easy answers, do not always seem to fit the situation.

Go to an art museum and make a tour. As you enter the gallery given over to modern, contemporary art, you will see a commentary on our age. The concern for order and symmetry, the interest in nature and its beauty, and the representation of life in meaningful symbols have been left behind in the galleries devoted to former ages. The great, screaming message of much of our art seems to be that there is no meaning at all. The tangled lines and indiscriminate blobs of color, the sculpture made of old automobile parts and bathtubs, which is timed to blow up as part of the show, these and other examples all point to a definite view of man and the world. Now I admit that I am a rank amateur in art history and appreciation, but the conclusion to which I have been driven is not mine only. The form of art today, or lack of it, is in itself symptomatic of a general mood.

Much of modern music expresses the same feeling of discordance and meaninglessness. The world pictured by these art forms and by much of contemporary literature is an ugly place of discord and lack of meaning.

Two questions need to be asked: Is this an accurate picture of the world, and does the Gospel have anything to say to this type of world?

Now, most of us don't spend our days in art museums or concert halls trying to analyze our age. To bring the problem closer to home, let's turn to another situation and ask, What is the meaning of God's love to a man working on an assembly line? Hour after hour, day after day, month after month, the same tedious repetition. And then home to the TV dinner and an evening before the television with its boring sameness. Has this type of life meaning or not: Does the Christian answer have anything at all to say to this person?

For centuries man lived as basically an agricultural being. He labored in one form or another to exist. "In the sweat of your face you shall eat bread till you return to the ground" (Gen. 3:19). Work was seen as an essential part of life, and faithfulness to one's work, diligence in its performance, was raised to the level of a virtue in Reformation ethics. Our age, however, poses a new problem as automation cuts into the work time of the laborer and makes him a person of enforced leisure. Can this leisure be used creatively and be made a time of growth and value, or will the pointlessness of mechanized labor be transferred to this area also? Does not the whole ethic of vocation, of labor, need to be rethought in the face of this century? In short, has the church anything to say to this problem? Simply to repeat words that fit an agrarian world will not suffice.

The whole matter of population explosion creates an additional bag of problems, not only for the politician and economist, but also for the church. Where should one stand on the problem of planned, responsible parenthood? Should the Christian work for laws that realistically face this issue by study and dissemination of birth control information, or should he simply wait for the race to breed itself off the face of the planet?

Geneticists tell us that it is only a matter of time before we will be able to so alter the genetic structure of the female ova that there need never again be mongoloid or other similar defectives born. Diabetes and other ills can also be prevented before birth by alteration of defective strains. What can we say to this activity? If such means are available, we must use them, unless of course we believe that God wills such suffering as is produced by the birth and life of a defective child. But who will decide the use of such tools? What kind of God-board will it be? And what about the next step, the actual breeding or alteration to improve the race itself? Even to mention such things shows us the depth of the moral problems that even now are upon us

Our cities are exploding. Thousands of farm and small-town people continue to flock to centers of population, looking for jobs and a better life. What they find is often something else. Where is the church to be? Can we afford to continue to follow our solid middle class people out into the suburbs, leaving our inner city churches to be furniture warehouses? The people of the inner city, many of them of depressed financial status, are also the objects of Christ's love and concern. Though they may never be able to have a self-supporting (the magic word) congregation, they must have the ministry of the church.

It is possible that the congregation is no longer a usable unit in some areas. Experiments are in process among the apartment dwellers in our big cities. The pastor moves from building to building, carrying the word of Christ to the people, rather than having them venture forth (itself an often dangerous move after dark). Our rural and suburban lands may need the congregation as a tool, but there must be an openness to experiment. Unless we can escape from the rural and suburban captivity of the church, we will never reach the heart of the cities. Christians, according to Christ, are to be fishers of men (Matt. 4:18-20). The insights of the lake and stream are rarely used in this type of angling, however. Instead of going where the fish are, no matter how arduous the path, we have often insisted on only dipping the line in our own pools, i.e. in our churches. And then we have wondered that there was not a catch. We must go where the fish are.

Closely allied with these problems is the racial issue. Is it sufficient for us to continue to assert that all men are equal *before God* without at least attempting to aid them to acquire equality *before the law* as well? It has sometimes been claimed that Sunday morning is the most segregated time of the week. Is it possible that this is indeed true? Our churches must be reformed in their thinking and action so that they no longer are tight little cultural and ethnic islands, warm and cozy inside, but presenting an unassailable front to the world. Christ died, not for our cozy clubs, but for the world, and the church must reach to all men. Some attempts are being made in this area, but only enough, I fear, to make us feel smug and satisfied. The real breakthrough which will open the church to all who wish to hear has not yet occurred.

The church needs also to recapture the picture of itself as the servant and not the master. The emergence of new national states throughout the world has often been accompanied by a reaction against the mission labors of the Christians in those areas. Missionary labors have been equated with imperialism of a new form. It must be admitted that some efforts on foreign fields fostered this understanding. The missionary was master who insisted upon making the natives over into little westerners as well as into Christians. The worker in foreign fields today has a different orientation. He sees himself as servant of the Word of God and of the people—a person who is the aid of the native Christians, not their master, whose goal is the establishment of an indigenous church, not the perpetuation of a western missionary island.

The role of the church as servant needs also to become more prominent on our own shores. The early church was marked by a willingness to spend itself freely so that the world might know Christ. Without special privilege or well-paved roads it marched ahead. Often the path of service to Christ and the world went by way of the cross. Can the American church ever freely move along such a path? Can it divest itself of its privileges sufficiently to become something other than a comfortable middle-class club? It must. If this means that we must give up, for example, our tax exempt status and pay our own way with the rest of the populace, then this is what we must do. Service, not lordship, is the mark of the Christian and the church (Matt. 20:20-28). Anything else will be contrary to the biblical witness and also repugnant to the modern world that has had quite enough of self-seeking, masterful movements.

These have only been a few suggestions as to the *type* of questions which we face as Christians today.

The basic problem remains the same, but this is an age when it manifests itself differently from the past. We must be open to the world and sensitive to its cries if we are indeed to be a witnessing church.

The Challenge to the Stereotype

A third suggestion: We must not allow the old stereotypes to persist.

On the one hand, we have the secular stereotype that pictures the Christian as some naive soul who believes God is an old man with a white beard sitting on a cloud somewhere. This image was expressed by the Soviet Cosmonaut who felt he had demolished the whole of the Christian message by the observation that "he had not seen God out there." This distorted picture should not be allowed to persist.

On the other hand, there is the Christian caricature of the scientist as some sort of demonic being who spends his days attempting to destroy the Christian faith. One must choose, says this caricature, between science and Christianity. This must also be put to rest.

It is true that a *purely materialistic* view of the world, whether espoused by scientist or others, is incompatible with the Christian faith. But scientific materialism is on the wane. The deeper science probes nature the less likely it seems that it can explain everything. On the Christian side of the science-Christianity problem, it must be asserted that "A faith is small indeed, if it fears reality."[4]

We must be willing to allow other fixed pictures to

be challenged also. It may well be, for example, that our understanding of church organization and structure will need to be reexamined. Protestants generally, in contrast to Roman Catholics, do not believe that any particular form of church government is given by God to be used always and everywhere. Despite this theoretical understanding regarding freedom of form, there has been a practical emphasis that seems to have made certain systems almost divine in themselves. Perhaps the Congregational, Presbyterian, or Episcopal forms are *not* the best means of spreading the Gospel in our day; we should at least be willing to examine what may be needed. The ultimate test, according to Luther, is whether the form is best suited for the spread of the Gospel. If this is our criterion, we may well find changes in this area also, especially as we seek to reach those in the inner city.

The Commitment to the Basic

In our quest, our faith, we must persist in the basic themes. Our message, our answer to the world's searching, does not consist of supposedly biblical pronouncements on geography, physics, chemistry, anthropology, and medicine. Our message is the good news *that God has not ceased in his quest, that he wills that we live in fellowship with him, and that only in this relationship can real hope and meaning be found.* The major themes of the reformers of the past are relevant today, for the divine-human relationship is characterized by trust, by obedience, and by discipleship. These themes and their implications can and must be made as vital to our century as they were to the sixteenth.

The suggestions made thus far have been concerned with the Christian as he faces the secular world. We should also be looking for the possibility of reform as we face other Christian bodies. We must cultivate a spirit of openness as we confront our brothers in Christ. This attitude should include a willingness to learn from them wherever they have something of value to teach. One of the great benefits of the ecumenical age is that we are now conversing with each other and are thus exposed to the best parts of the traditions of others. There is much we can learn.

We can learn to face the ecumenical encounter itself with hope and confidence. The movement is a natural result of the scriptural concern of the Protestant reformers and of the view of the church as a body embracing all who are in a faith-relationship with Christ. The notion that *only* those who believe, *in every detail,* as *I do* are Christian is really a sectarian-Protestant, and, up to a few years ago, a Roman Catholic view. It is not the position of progressive Catholics today.

In this learning period Catholics have benefited from contact with Protestant biblical studies which have not been hindered by the same type of dogmatic presuppositions and rigidity as have their own. This type of contact has been of acknowledged value to Rome, and to the whole theological endeavor. They have been willing to learn, and as a result their church is moving into the modern world. Catholics have also discovered much about church life in a pluralistic society where religious freedom is the rule. They could not have learned this from the reformers themselves, but from later developments within Protestantism. This has caused a whole new evaluation of the place of the church in society and of the necessity of freedom for the individual believer.

This openness to the world, the concern for actual reform, to use Pope Paul's term, which we see in certain parts of Catholicism should jolt Protestants loose from their concrete ties to the past. If the supposedly "monolithic" (a favorite Protestant word) Catholic Church is moving, how can the "dynamic" bodies of Protestantism remain at dead center? The Catholic Church is beginning to move because it is opening itself up both to the world and to other Christian bodies. It is willing to learn and listen.

Protestants must also be listening churches. We can contribute of our own wealth to others. To illustrate briefly: The Reformed churches and their concern for the disciplined Christan life; the Methodists with their emphasis on sanctification; the Lutherans with their understanding of justification by faith and the life of trust—all can enrich others by their own particular major themes. The Eastern Orthodox understanding of the Lord's Supper as being essentially the reenactment of the resurrection, not the passion and death of Christ, can enrich all members of the Christian family. Instead of concentrating only on the sorrow and suffering caused by sin, one sees also the glory and power of the risen Christ. The Supper becomes a time of exultation and joy, rather than only a time of penitential sorrow.

We must listen and learn from our Catholic brothers also. The best in progressive Catholicism with its concern for renewal in worship, its fresh interest in biblical and historical research, and above all its openness to the world and other Christian bodies should prod Protestants to action, and could enrich their Christian lives.

Our immediate goal as we face other Christians in this ecumenical era should be to take advantage of the new atmosphere. The age of polemics has passed, and we must now "work while it is day," and make maximum use of the current situation. We must press on in our discussions, avoiding the extremes of easy optimism and polemical defensiveness, working for the mutual understanding, respect, and love which should characterize life in the body of Christ. This "pressing on" is in itself a part of the continuing reformation of the church.

As we face the modern world, we must be aware of how in some ways it is radically different from the past, while in others it is basically the same. This is a secular and pluralistic world, its thought forms, questions, and language differ from the past. Yet it is also a world in which men are still looking for the meaning, the significance of life. While some continue to look to themselves, to materialism, humanism, and other "isms" by the score, these answers have not sufficed. Only as man's religious quest reveals that it is

God who is searching for him, only then, in a life of relationship, is meaning found.

This life in relationship is the answer which Christians hold up to the searching man of any age. To make this relevant to the twentieth century is our task. To do this, the church must be in a continual state of reexamination and reformation.

The church must always be reformed.

> Farewell, kindly reader, and if you benefit at all from my labors, help me with your prayers before God our Father.[5]

Footnotes

[1] Luther, *The Large Catechism, op. cit.,* p. 412.

[2] Attributed to William Norman Ewer, cf. *Concise Oxford Dictionary of Quotations* (London: Oxford University Press, 1964), p. 83

[3] Malcolm Boyd, *Are You Running With Me, Jesus?* (New York, etc.: Holt, Rinehart and Winston, 1965), p. 22.

[4] Stanley Beck, *The Simplicity of Science* (Garden City, N.Y.. Doubleday, 1959), p. 193.

[5] Calvin, *op. cit.,* I, p. 5.

Bibliography

Beck, Stanley, *The Simplicity of Science*. Garden City, New York: Doubleday, 1959.

Boyd, Malcolm, *Are You Running with Me, Jesus?* New York: Holt, Rinehart and Winston, 1965.

Concise Oxford Dictionary of Quotations. London: Oxford University Press, 1964.

Herschberger, G. F. (ed.) *The Recovery of the Anabaptist Vision*. Scottdale, Pa.: Herald Press, 1957.

Klassen, H. *Mennonite Quarterly Review*, July, 1959, XXXIII, No. 3 p. 187.

Lehmann, Paul. "Protestantism in a Post Christian World," *Christianity and Crisis*, 1962, XXII, No. 1, p. 7.

Luther, Martin. *D. Martin Luthers Werke, Kritische Gesamtausgabe* Weimar: H. Bohlau, 1883-1947.

———*Works of Martin Luther*. 6 Vols. Philadelphia: Muhlenberg Press, 1930-43.

———*Luther's Works*. J. Pelikan and H. T. Lehmann (eds.) 55 Vols. (not complete). Philadelphia & St. Louis: Fortress Press and Concordia Pub. House, 1957—.

McLelland, J. C., *The Reformation and Its Significance Today*. Philadelphia: Westminster Press, 1962.

McNeill, J. T. *The History and Character of Calvinism*. New York: Oxford University Press, 1957.

———(ed.) *The Institutes of Christian Religion* by John Calvin. Philadelphia: Westminster Press, 1960.

Pastor, Ludwig, *The History of the Popes, from the Close of the Middle Ages*. 24 Vols. London: Kegan Paul, French, Trubner and Co., Ltd., 1924.

Pauck, Wilhelm, *The Heritage of the Reformation*. Glencoe, Ill.: Glencoe Free Press, 1961.

Pusey, E. (ed.) *The Confessions of St. Augustine*. New York: Pocket Books Inc., 1951.

Scheel, Otto. *Dokumente zu Luthers Entwicklung*. Tübingen: J. C. B. Mohr, 1930.

Skydsgaard, K. E. (ed.). *The Papal Council and the Gospel*. Minneapolis: Augsburg Publishing House, 1961.

Tappert, T. (trans. and ed.). *The Book of Concord*. Philadelphia: Muhlenberg Press, 1959.

Williams, G., and A. Mergal. (eds.). *Spiritual and Anabaptist Writers*. Philadelphia: Westminster, 1957.